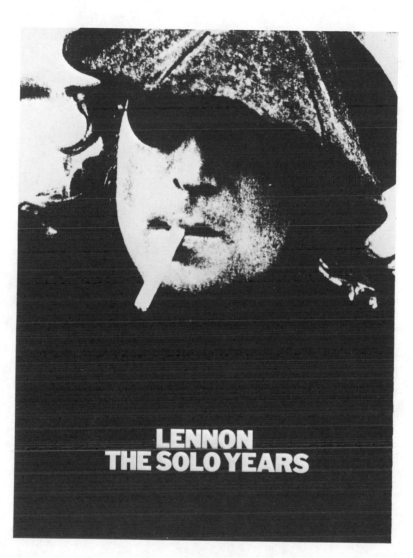

Art Director Pearce Marchbank
Designed by Carroll & Dempsey Ltd.

HAL·LEONARD® CORPORATION

7777 W. BLUEMOUND RD. P.O. BOX 13819 MILWAUKEE, WI 53213

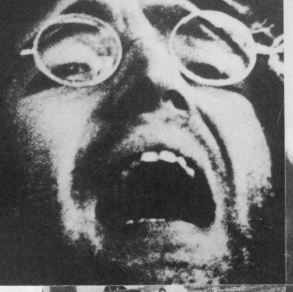

PLAYING GUIDE

The songs in this Hal Leonard EASY GUITAR collection are presented with easy-to-read music and lyrics. Chord frames are given to aid the player with left-hand fingerings; however, intermediate and advanced players should feel free to use bar chords or other more advanced chord forms.

These arrangements reflect the style of the original recordings and are presented in easy-to-play keys. You may wish to sing some songs an octave lower than written and/or use a capo to adjust the level to your voice range.

Below the title you will find **strums** and **finger picks** which can be used with each song. See page 7 for an explanation of these symbols.

SAMPLE

IMAGINE

WORDS & MUSIC BY JOHN LENNON

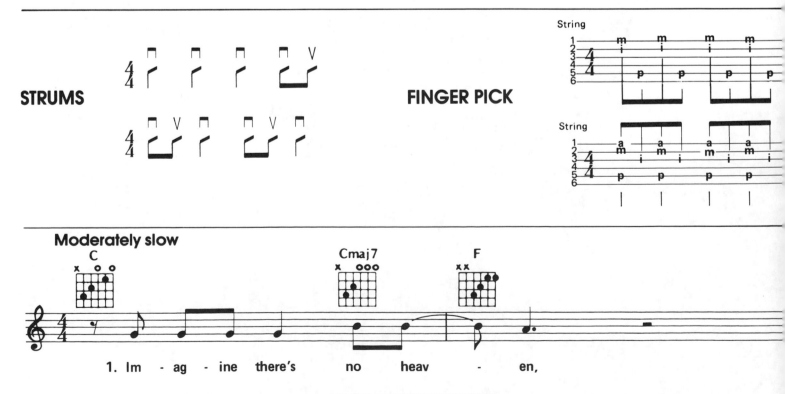

STRUMS

FINGER PICK

Moderately slow

1. Im - ag - ine there's no heav - en,

STRUMS AND FINGER PICKS

Finger picks and strums are written out at the top of each arrangement. The system used throughout all **Hal Leonard Guitar** books is explained below

FINGER PICKING

The fingers are named p, i, m, a in the following manner:

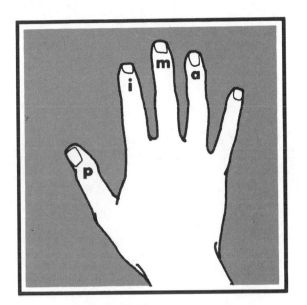

- The thumb (p) plucks strings 4, 5, or 6 depending upon which string is the root of the chord. This motion is a downward stroke. Use the left side of the thumb and thumbnail.
- The other fingers (i, m, a) pluck the string in an upward stroke with the fleshy tip of the finger and fingernail.
- The index finger (i) always plucks string 3.
- The middle finger (m) always plucks string 2.
- The ring finger (a) always plucks string 1.

The thumb and each finger must pluck only one string per stroke and not brush over several strings. (This would be a strum.) Let the strings ring throughout the duration of the chord.

Strums

The Strum symbols and their meanings are as follows:

       ⊓ — Down stroke
       V — Up stroke
       X — Dampening with the hand

THE BALLAD OF JOHN AND YOKO

WORDS & MUSIC BY JOHN LENNON AND PAUL McCARTNEY

STRUMS

FINGER PICK

Brightly

(Instrumental)

1. Stand - ing in the dock at South - amp - ton,
2. Final - ly made the plane in - to Pa - ris,
3. Pa - ris to the Am - ster - dam Hil - ton,
4. Made a light - ning trip to Vi - en - na,
5. Caught the ear - ly plane back to Lon - don,

trying to get to Hol - land or France. The
hon - ey - moon - ing down by the Seine. Pe - ter
talk - ing in our beds for a week. The
eat - ing choc' - late cake in a bag. The
fif - ty a - corns tied in a sack. The

man in the mac said you've got to go back; you know they
Brown called to say, you can make it O. K., you can get
news - pa - pers said, say what're you do - ing in bed, I said we're
news - pa - pers said, she's gone to his head, they
men from the press said we wish you suc - cess, it's

Last night the wife said, Oh boy, when you're dead you

won't take noth-ing with you but your soul._____ Think!

The way things are go - ing,_____

they're going to cru - ci - fy_____ me.

(Instrumental)

IMAGINE
WORDS & MUSIC BY JOHN LENNON

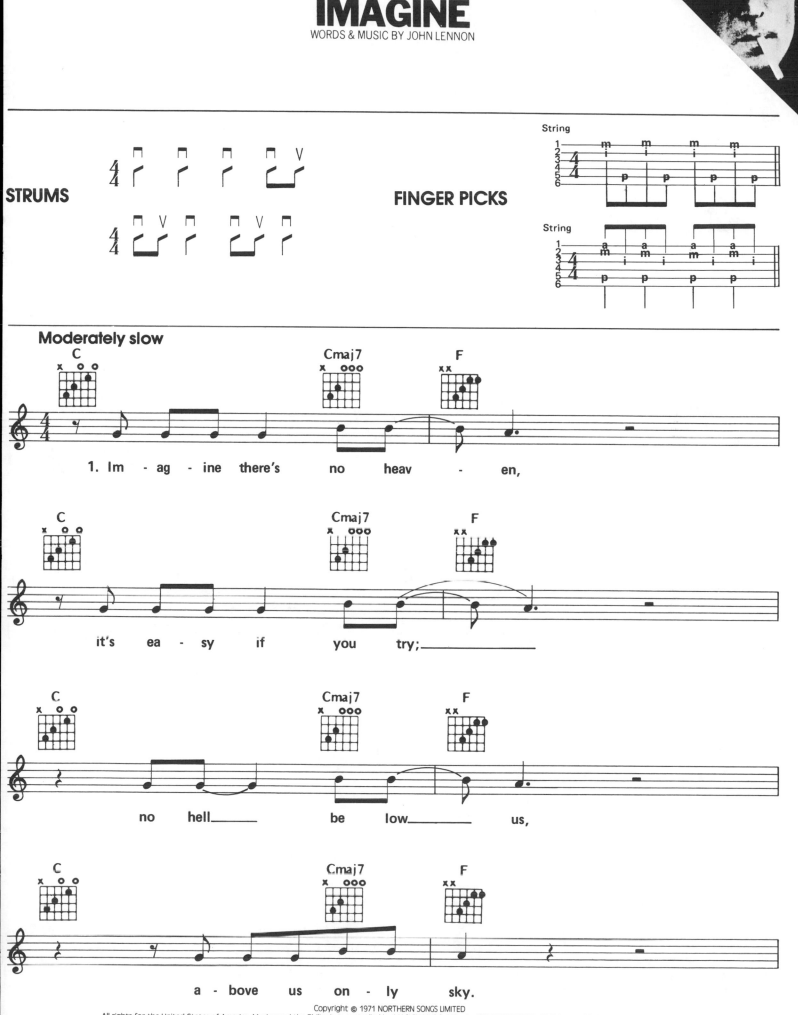

STRUMS

FINGER PICKS

Moderately slow

C   Cmaj7   F

1. Im - ag - ine there's no heav - en,

C   Cmaj7   F

it's ea - sy if you try;____

C   Cmaj7   F

no hell____ be low____ us,

C   Cmaj7   F

a - bove us on - ly sky.

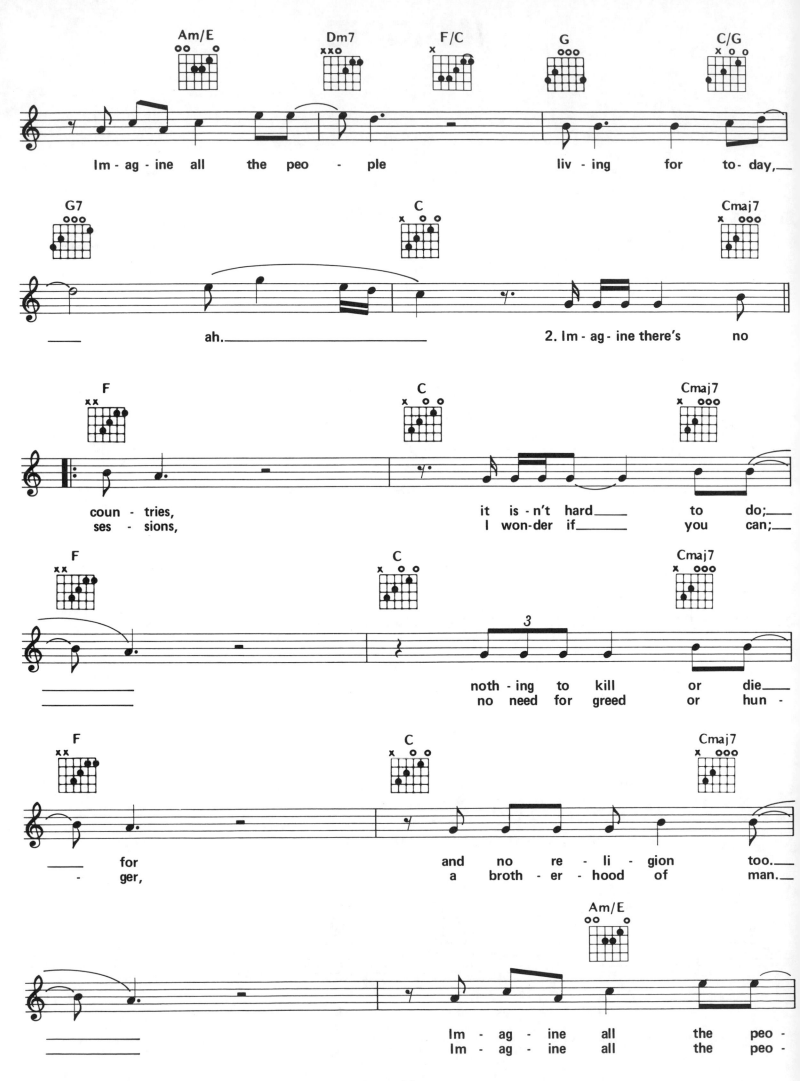

be as one. *(Instrumental)*   3. Im-ag-ine no pos - be as one._____

13

GIVE PEACE A CHANCE

WORDS & MUSIC BY JOHN LENNON AND PAUL McCARTNEY

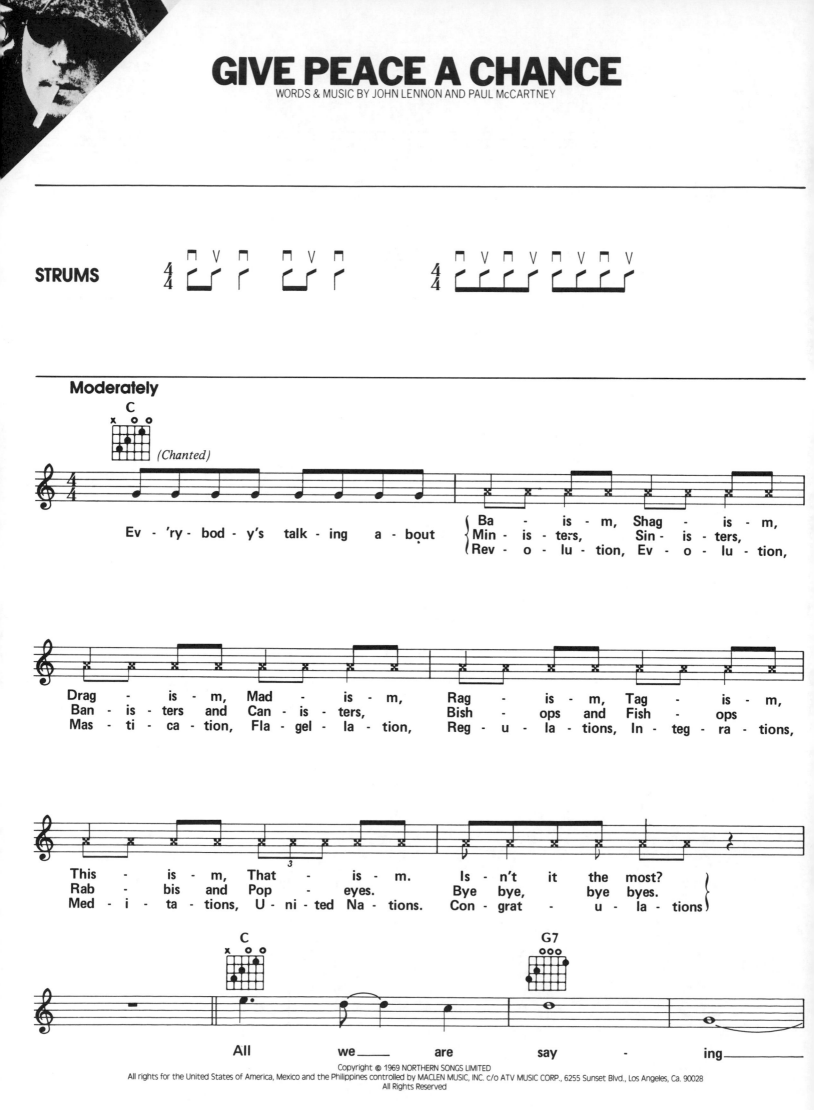

Additional Lyrics

4. Ev'rybody's talking about John and Yoko, Timmy Leary, Rosemary, Tommy Smothers,
   Bobby Dylan, Tommy Cooper, Derek Taylor, Norman Mailer, Alan Ginsberg, Hare Krishna;
   Hare, Hare Krishna.

POWER TO THE PEOPLE

WORDS & MUSIC BY JOHN LENNON

Moderate March Tempo

Pow-er to the peo - ple, pow-er to the peo - ple.

Pow-er to the peo - ple, pow-er to the peo - ple.

pow - er to the peo - ple, pow - er to the peo - ple, right o

1. You say you want a rev - o - lu - tion, we'd bet - te
2. A mil - lion work - ers work - in' for noth - ing, you bet - te
3. I gon - na ask __ you com - rades and broth - ers, how do yo
4. (Instrumental)

get   on   right   a - way. _____   Well, let's get
give   them what they real   ly   own. _____   We got - ta
treat   your old   wom - an back home?_____   She's got - ta

on   your   feet, ___   end of the   street, ___
put   you   down___ when we come   in - to_____ town, ___   sing - ing:
be   her - self ____ so she can   give us_____ help, ___

(Instrumental)_____   Oh,   well: ___

Repeat and Fade

Pow - er   to   the   peo - ple,   pow - er   to   the peo -

- ple.   Pow - er   to   the   peo - ple,

pow - er   to   the   peo - ple, right   on. _____

17

COLD TURKEY

WORDS & MUSIC BY JOHN LENNON

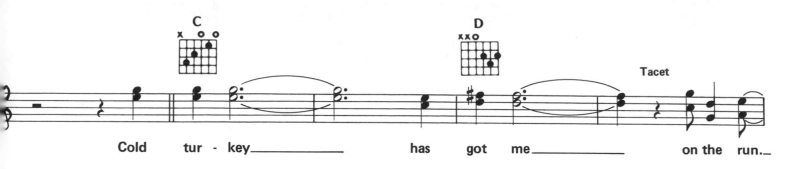

Cold tur - key_____ has got me_____ on the run._____

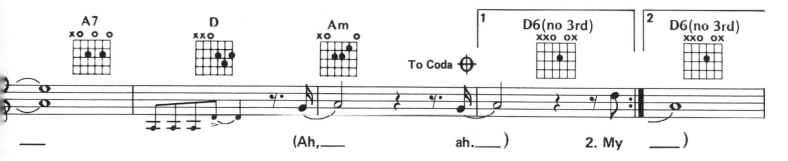

_____ (Ah,___ ah.___) 2. My ___)

Ah,_____ oh._____ Oo,_____ oh._____

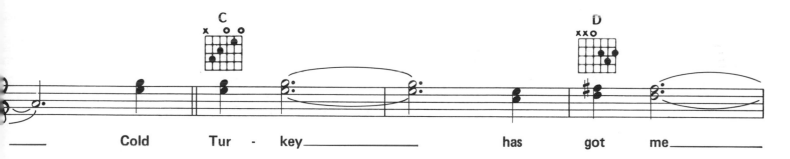

_____ Cold Tur - key_____ has got me_____

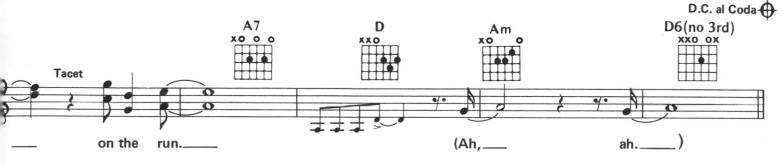

D.C. al Coda

_____ on the run._____ (Ah,___ ah.___)

Repeat 49 times adding shouts of "oh," "ah,"
"oo," "no," yells, moans, groans, shrieks, etc.

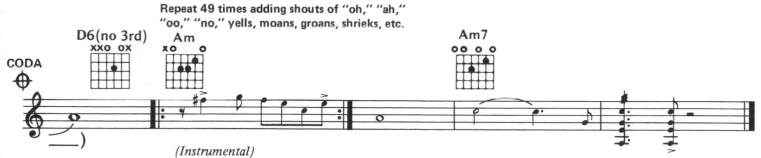

CODA

___)

(Instrumental)

WHATEVER GETS YOU THRU THE NIGHT

THE NIGHT

WORDS & MUSIC BY JOHN LENNON

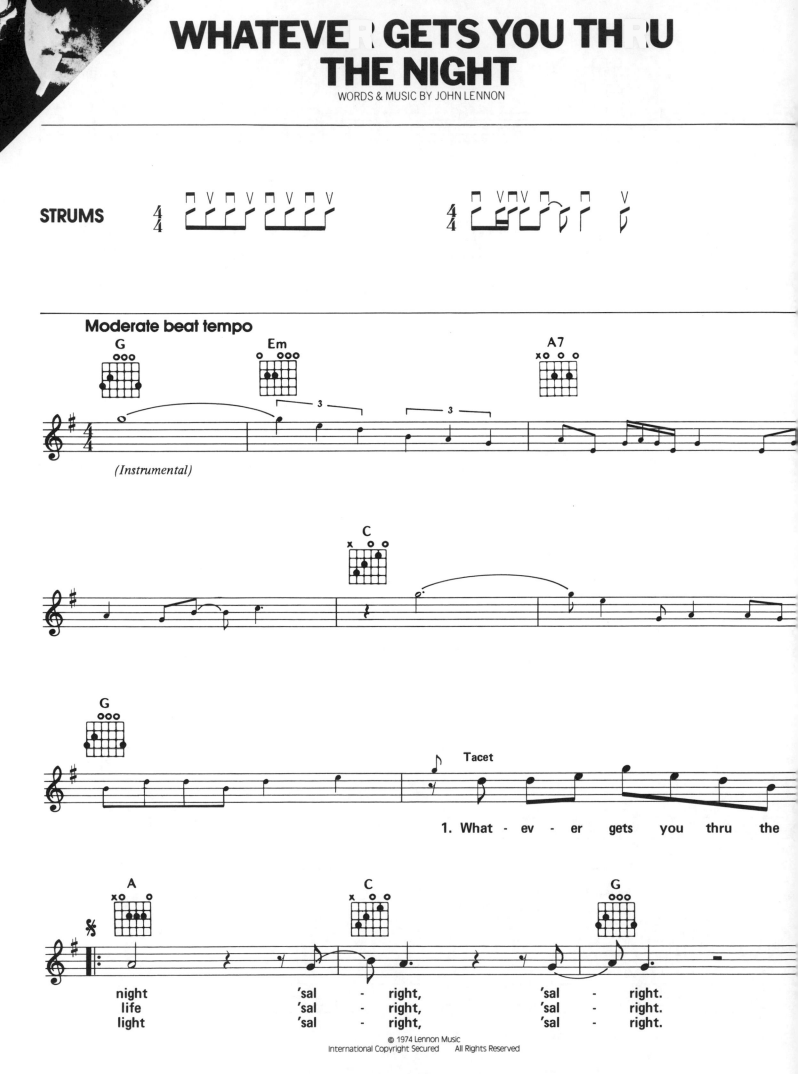

It's your mon - ey or your life;   'sal - right,   'sal -
Do it wrong or do it right;   'sal - right,   'sal -
Out the blue or out of sight;   'sal - right,   'sal -

- right.   Don't need a sword to cut thru'
- right.   Don't need a watch to waste your
- right.   Don't need a gun to blow your

flow - ers, _____   oh no, _____   oh no. _____
time, _____
mind, _____

2. What - ev - er gets you thru' the   (Instrumental)

Hold me dar - lin', come on

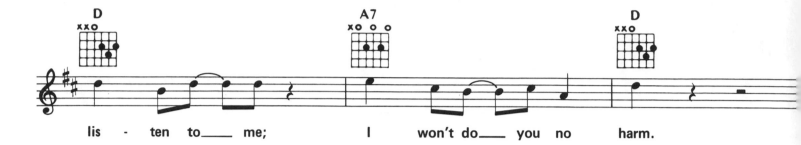

lis - ten to___ me; I won't do___ you no harm.

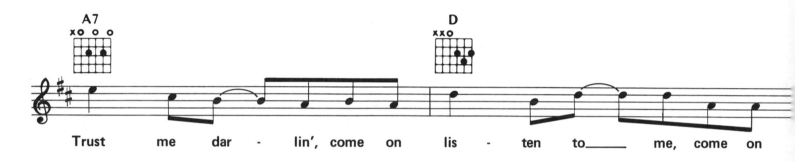

Trust me dar - lin', come on lis - ten to___ me, come on

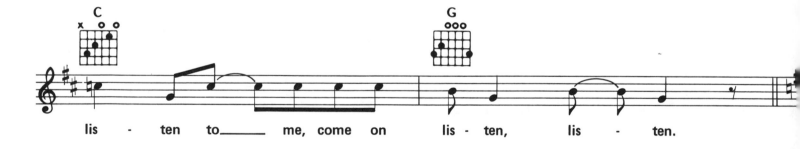

lis - ten to___ me, come on lis - ten, lis - ten.

(Instrumental)

Tacet

D.S. 𝄋 (no repeat) and fa
on last Instrumental secti

3. What - ev - er gets you to the

22

MY MUMMY'S DEAD

WORDS & MUSIC BY JOHN LENNON

STRUMS

$\frac{4}{4}$

$\frac{4}{4}$

FINGER PICK

String

Moderately, with great simplicity

D   Asus4   D   Asus4

My mum-my's dead. _____ I can't get it through my head, _____

D   Asus4

_____ though it's been so man-y years. _____ My mum-my's

D   Asus4   D

dead; _____ I can't ex - plain so much pain,

I could nev - er show it. My mum-my's dead.

MOTHER

WORDS & MUSIC BY JOHN LENNON

STRUMS

FINGER PICKS String

String

Slowly

1. Moth - er,_____ you had   me_____ but I nev - er had
2. Fa - ther,_____ you left   me_____ but I nev - er left
3. Chil - dren,_____ don't____   do_____ what__ I__have

you._____
you._____
done;_____

I _____ want-ed   you,____   you did-n't want
I _____ need-ed   you,____   you did-n't need
I _____ could-n't   walk____   and I tried to

me.
me. }
run.)

So___   I,_____

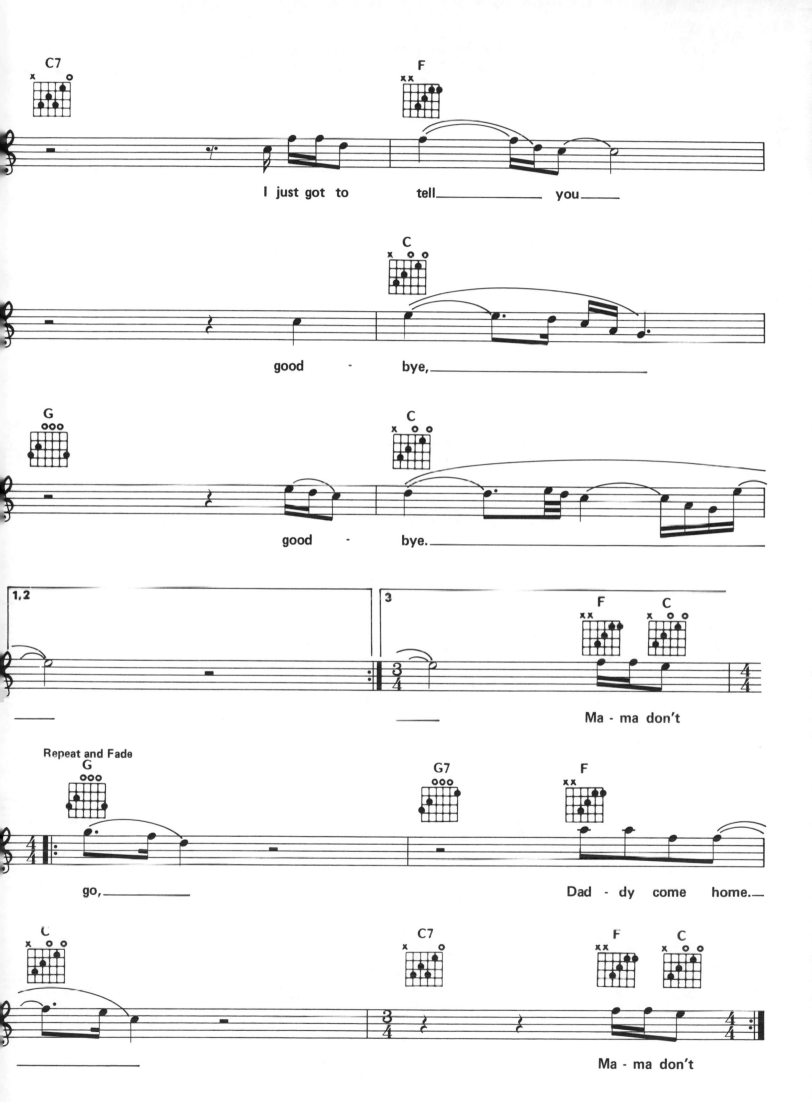

I just got to   tell_____ you_____

good - bye,_____

good - bye._____

Ma - ma don't

Repeat and Fade

go,_____

Dad - dy come home.__

Ma - ma don't

25

INSTANT KARMA
WORDS & MUSIC BY JOHN LENNON

What on earth you tryin' to do? It's up to you, yeah you.___
Who on earth d'you think you are, a su-per star? Well, al-

___ right you are! Well, we all shine

on,___ like the moon___ and the stars___ and the sun.___ Well, we

D.C. al Coda

all shine on.___ Ev-'ry-one,_ come on.___

CODA

Sure-ly not to live in pain and fear. Why on earth are you there,_

___ when you're ev-'ry-where?_ Come and get your share._ Well, we

27

all shine on,_____ like the moon____and the stars____ and the

sun._____ Well, we all shine on._____ Come on and on and on,

on._____ Yeah, yeah. Al - right.

Ah ha, ah._____ Well, we

on and on.____ Well, we on and on.____ Well, we all shine

on,_____ like the moon____and the stars____ and the sun._____ Well, we

THE LUCK OF THE IRISH

WORDS & MUSIC BY JOHN LENNON AND YOKO ONO

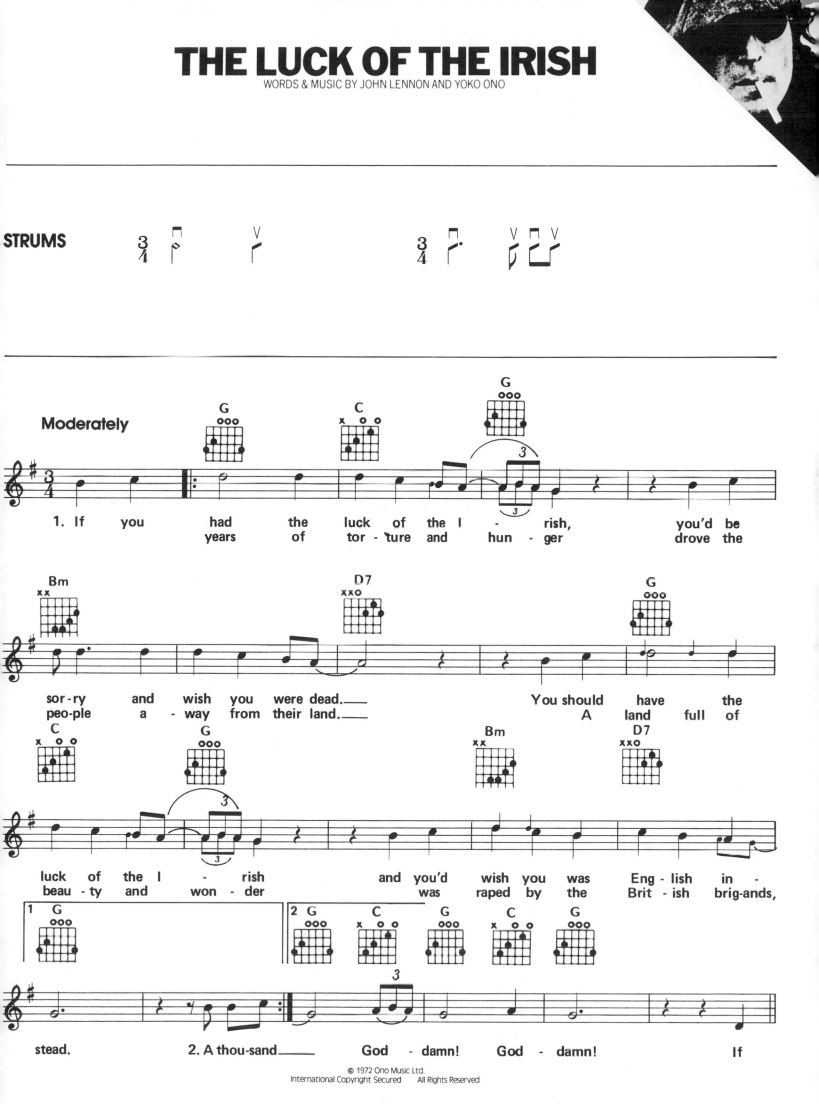

WOMAN

WORDS & MUSIC BY JOHN LENNON

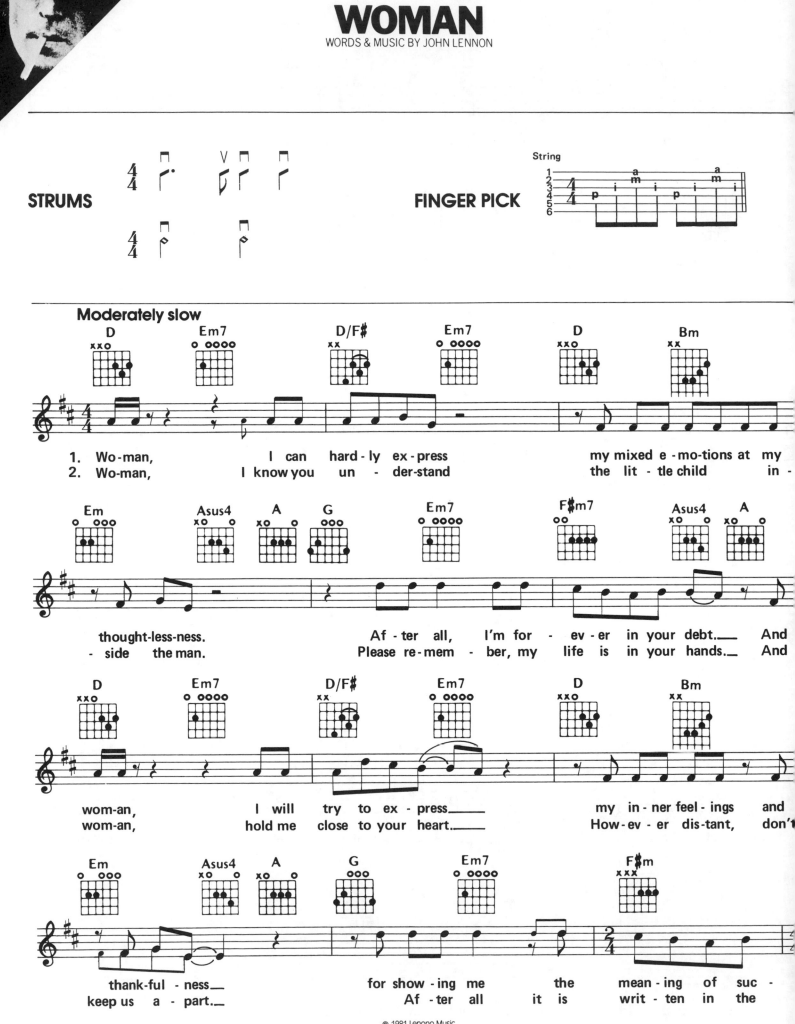

LOVE

WORDS & MUSIC BY JOHN LENNON

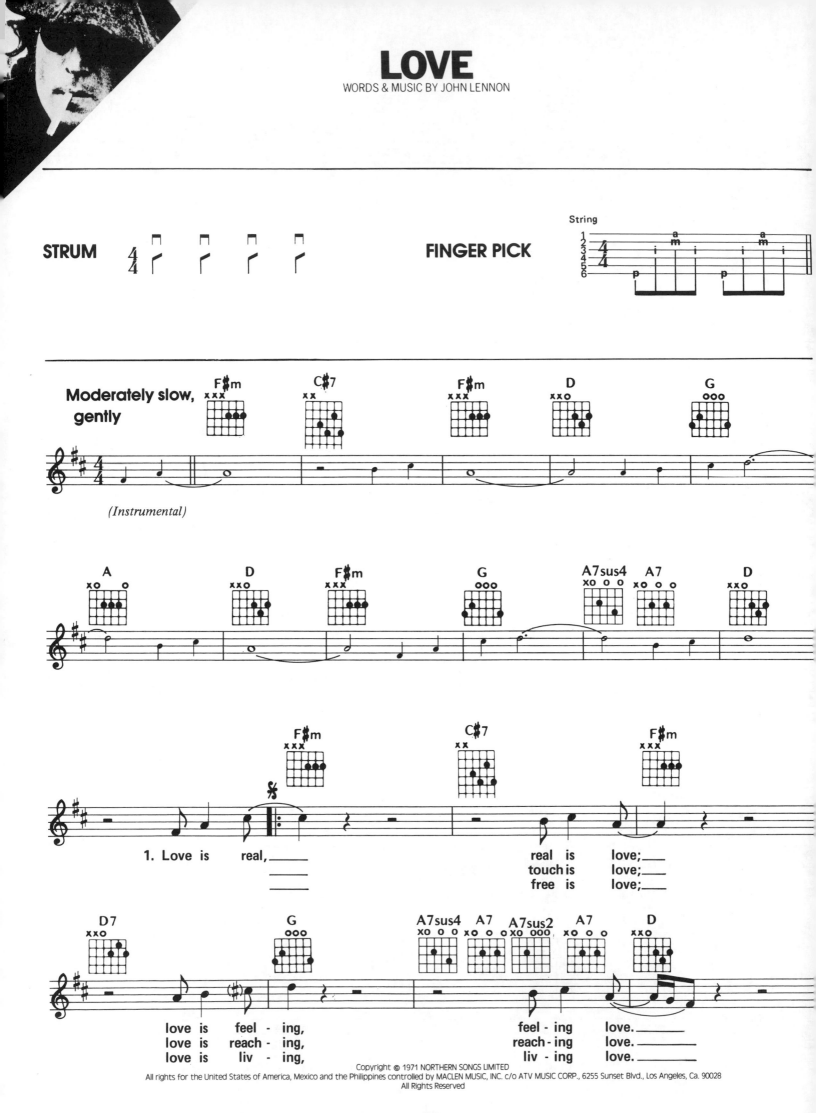

STRUM

FINGER PICK

Moderately slow, gently

(Instrumental)

1. Love is real,_____ real is love;_____
   touch is love;_____
   free is love;_____

love is feel-ing, feel-ing love._____
love is reach-ing, reach-ing love._____
love is liv-ing, liv-ing love._____

I'M LOSING YOU

WORDS & MUSIC BY JOHN LENNON

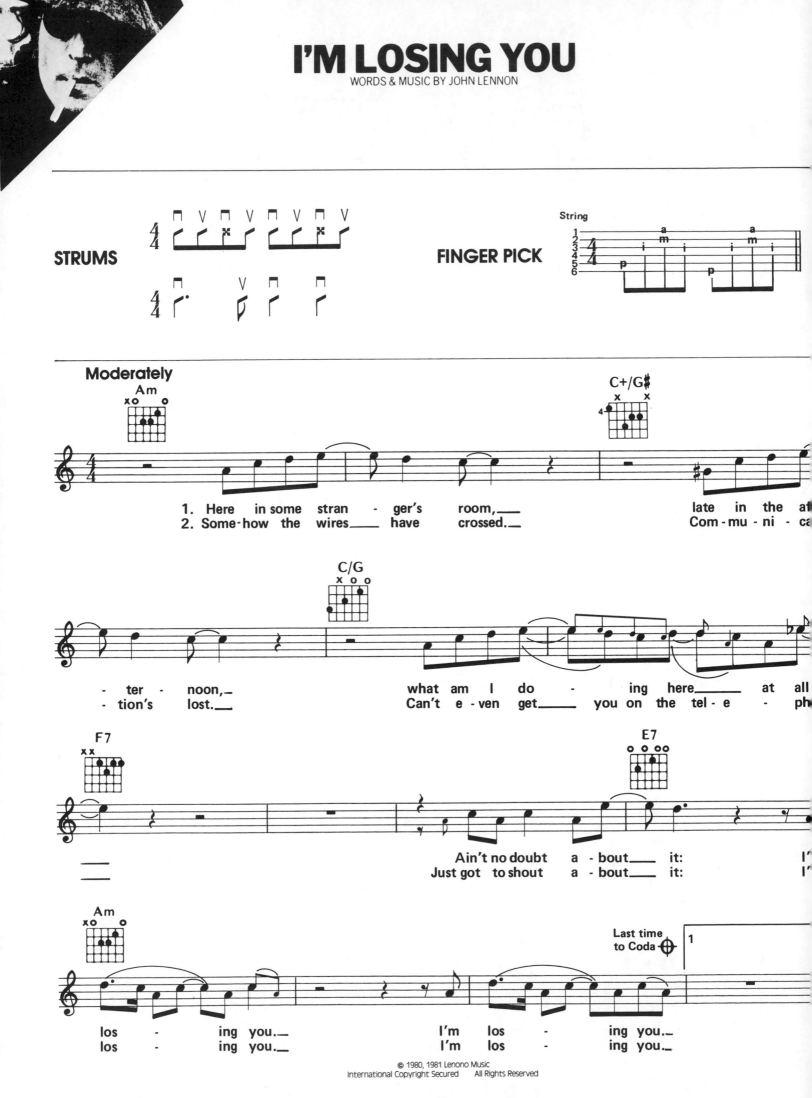

STRUMS

FINGER PICK

Moderately

Am   C+/G#

1. Here in some stran - ger's room,___   late in the af
2. Some-how the wires___ have crossed.___   Com - mu - ni - ca

C/G

- ter - noon,___   what am I do - ing here   at all
- tion's lost.___   Can't e - ven get___ you on the tel - e - ph

F7   E7

Ain't no doubt a - bout___ it: I'
Just got to shout a - bout___ it: I'

Am

Last time
to Coda   1

los - ing you.___   I'm los - ing you.___
los - ing you.___   I'm los - ing you.___

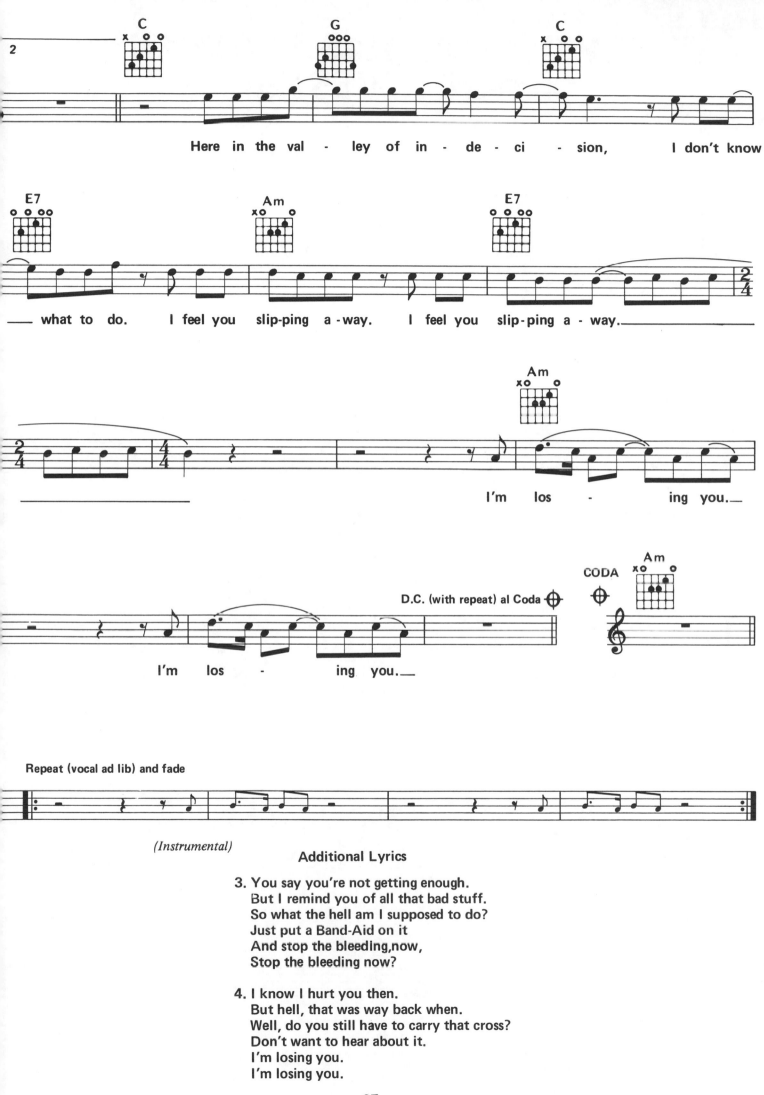

2

C   G   C

Here in the val - ley of in - de - ci - sion, I don't know

E7   Am   E7

— what to do. I feel you slip-ping a - way. I feel you slip-ping a - way.—

Am

I'm los - ing you.—

D.C. (with repeat) al Coda ⊕   ⊕   CODA   Am

I'm los - ing you.—

Repeat (vocal ad lib) and fade

(Instrumental)

Additional Lyrics

3. You say you're not getting enough.
   But I remind you of all that bad stuff.
   So what the hell am I supposed to do?
   Just put a Band-Aid on it
   And stop the bleeding, now,
   Stop the bleeding now?

4. I know I hurt you then.
   But hell, that was way back when.
   Well, do you still have to carry that cross?
   Don't want to hear about it.
   I'm losing you.
   I'm losing you.

EVERY MAN HAS A WOMAN WHO LOVES HIM

WORDS & MUSIC BY YOKO ONO

STRUMS

Moderately

1. Ev-'ry man_____ has a wom-an who loves him,____ rain or shine
2. Ev-'ry wom-an_____ has a man__ who loves her,____ rise or fall

____ or__ life_____ ____ or death.____
____ or her life_____ and in death.____

(Instrumental)

If he finds_____ her in this life - time,
If she finds_____ him in this life - time,

he will know_____ when he press - es his ear to her breast.
she will know_____ when she looks in - to his eyes.

Why do I roam_____ when I know you're the one?____
Why do I roam_____ when I know you're the one?____

Why do I laugh_____ when I feel like cry - ing?
Why do I run_____ when I feel like hold -

ing you?__ Ev-'ry man_____ has a

wom-an who loves him.____ If he finds_____ her in this life - time,

he will know. (Instrumental)

Repeat and Fade

(Instrumental)

REMEMBER

WORDS & MUSIC BY JOHN LENNON

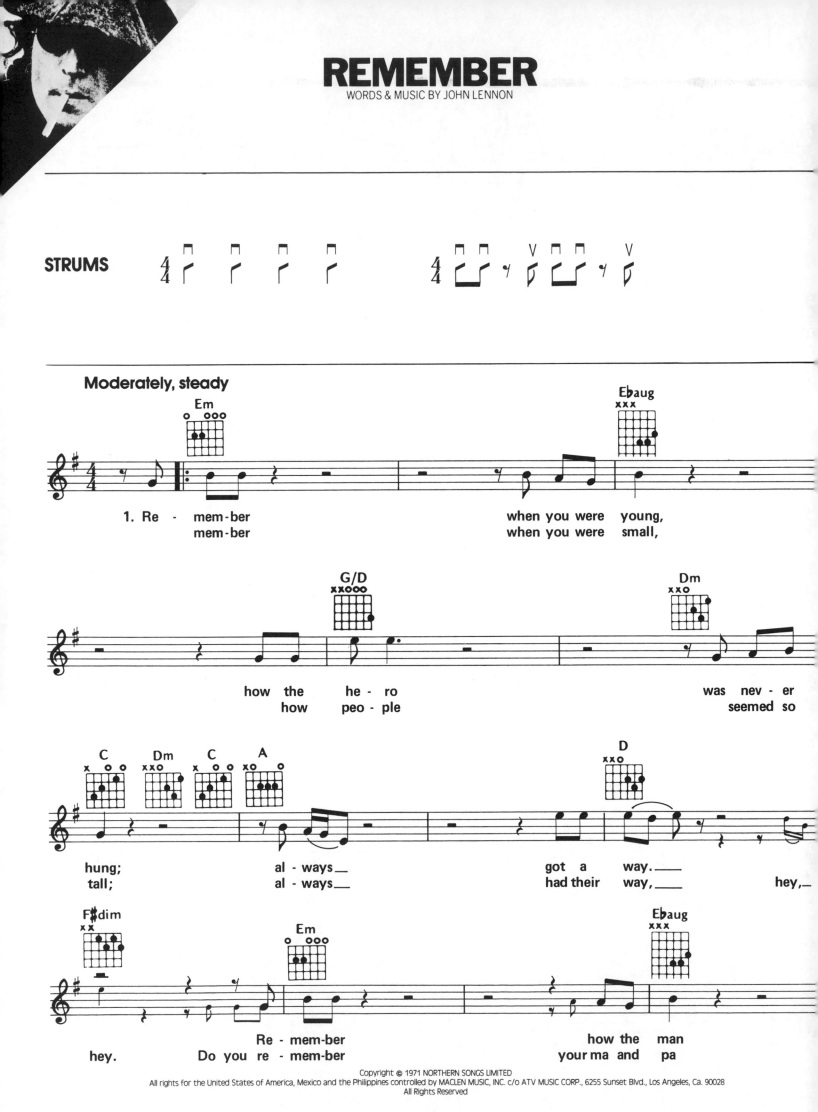

STRUMS

Moderately, steady

1. Re - mem - ber
mem - ber

when you were young,
when you were small,

how the he - ro
how peo - ple

was nev - er
seemed so

hung;
tall;

al - ways
al - ways

got a way.
had their way, hey,

hey.
Do you re - mem - ber

Re - mem - ber
how the man
your ma and pa

re-mem-ber _____ to - day, _____ hey.
re-mem-ber _____ to - day, _____ hey.

N.C. Don't feel sor - ry _____

'bout the way it's gone, _____ don't you wor -

ry _____ 'bout what you've done. _____ 2. Just re-

No, re - mem-ber, re - mem-ber

the fifth of No - vem-ber. (Explosion)

WATCHING THE WHEELS

WORDS & MUSIC BY JOHN LENNON

STRUMS

Moderately, in 2

(Instrumental)

1. Peo-ple say I'm cra - zy   do - in' what I'm
2. Peo-ple say I'm la - zy,   dream-in' my
3. Peo-ple ask-ing ques - tions,   lost in con -

do - in'.___   Well, they
life___ a - way.___   Well, they
fu - sion.___   Well, I

give me all kinds___ of warn - ings   to save me from
give me all kinds___ of ad - vice   de - signed to en -
tell them there's___ no prob - lem,   on - ly so -

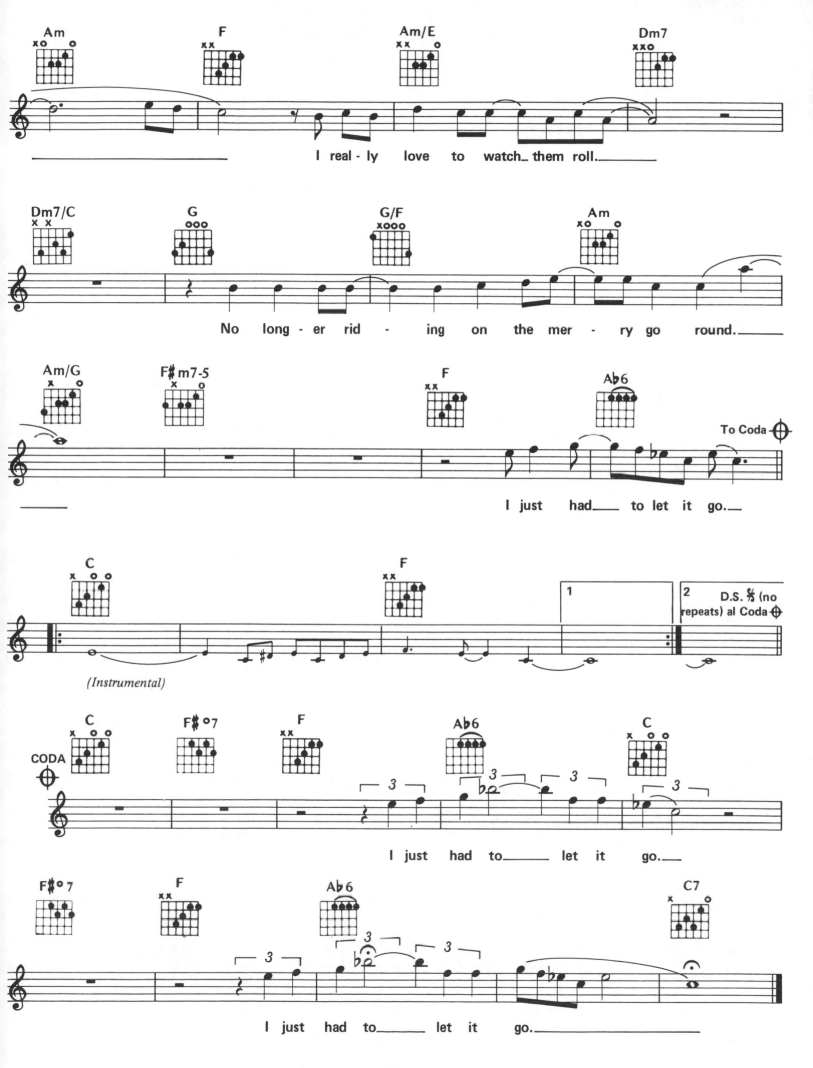

I real-ly love to watch them roll.

No long-er rid - ing on the mer - ry go round.

I just had to let it go.

(Instrumental)

I just had to let it go.

I just had to let it go.

KISS, KISS, KISS

WORDS & MUSIC BY YOKO ONO

Kiss,   kiss,   kiss,   kiss me   love.
Touch,   touch,   touch,   kiss touch me   love.

I'm   bleed - ing   in - side._____
I'm   shak - ing   in - side._____

It's   a   long,   long   sto - ry   to   tell _____ and
It's   that   faint,   faint sound of   the   child - hood   bell,

I   can   on - ly   show   you   my   hell.
ring - ing   in____   my   soul.

(Instrumental)

Kiss,   kiss,   kiss,   kiss me,

love.   Just   one   kiss   kiss will   do.

ISOLATION

WORDS & MUSIC BY JOHN LENNON

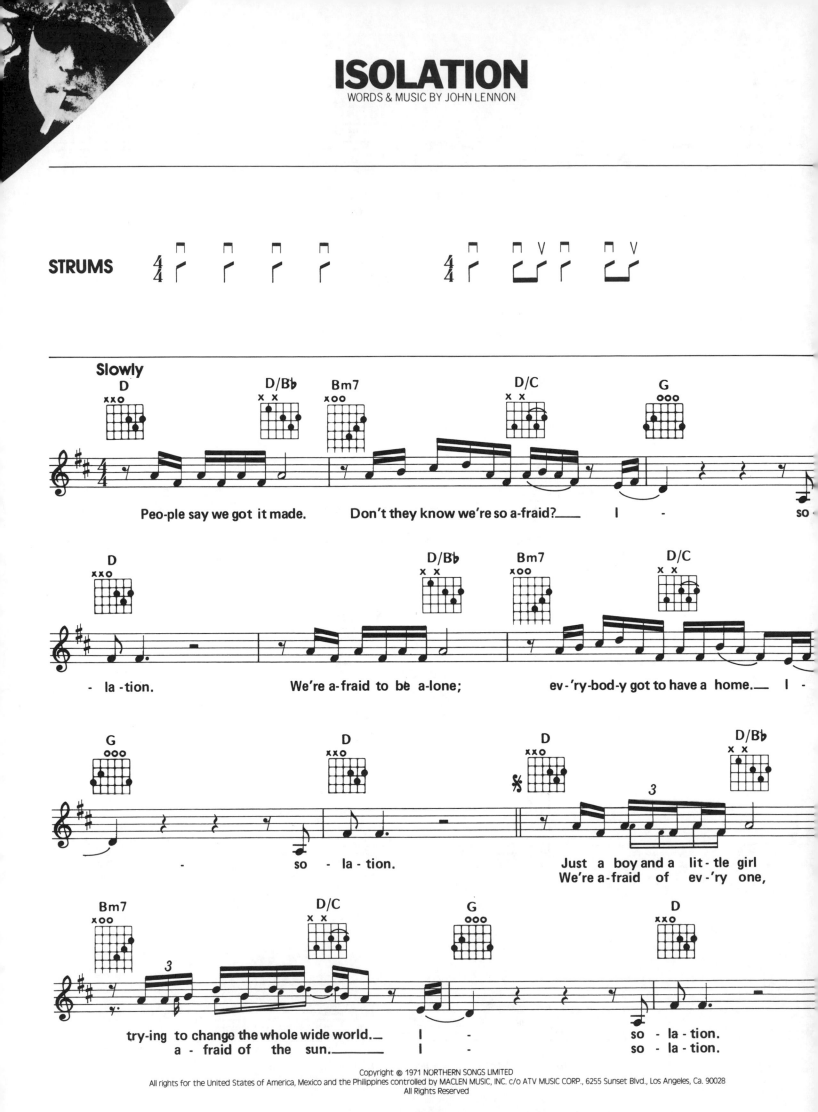

STRUMS

Peo-ple say we got it made. Don't they know we're so a-fraid?____ I -

so-

- la -tion.

We're a-fraid to be a-lone;

ev-'ry-bod-y got to have a home.____ I -

- so - la - tion.

Just a boy and a lit-tle girl
We're a-fraid of ev-'ry one,

try-ing to change the whole wide world.____ I -
a-fraid of the sun.____ I -

so - la - tion.
so - la - tion.

MIND GAMES

WORDS & MUSIC BY JOHN LENNON

GOD

WORDS & MUSIC BY JOHN LENNON

DRUMS

FINGER PICK

Moderately

1.2. God is a con-cept

by which we

meas- ure __ our __ pain.

(Instrumental)

I'll say it a - gain. __

Yeah, __ yeah, __ yeah.

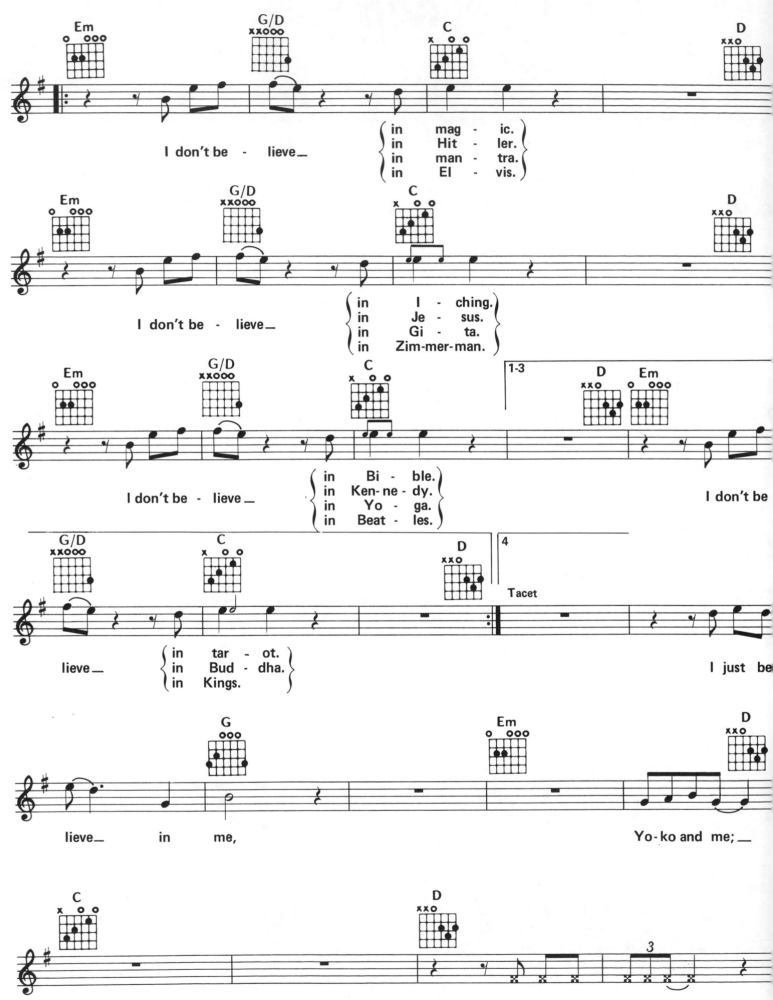

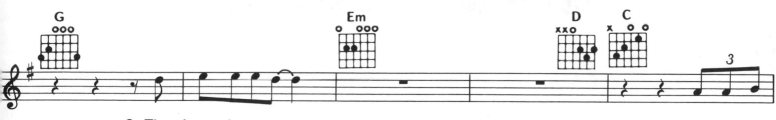

3. The dream is o - ver;__ what can I

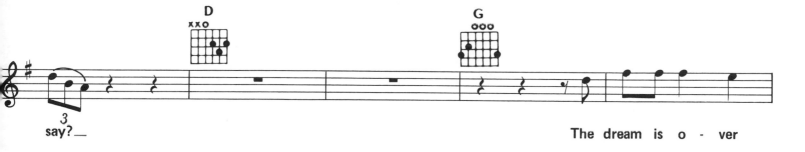

say?__ The dream is o - ver

yes - ter - day. _____

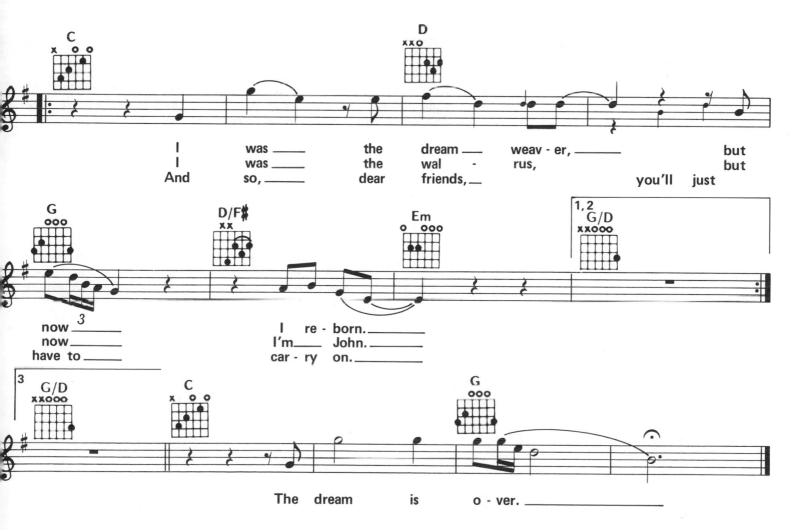

I   was ____ the   dream ____ weav - er, _____ but
I   was ____ the   wal - rus, ____ but
And so, ____ dear   friends, ____ you'll just

now _____ I   re - born. _____
now ____ I'm ____ John. _____
have to ____ car - ry on. _____

The   dream   is   o - ver. _____

WORKING CLASS HERO

WORDS & MUSIC BY JOHN LENNON

STRUMS

FINGER PICK

Moderately fast

Am ... G ... Am

1. As soon as you're born____ they make you feel small____
hurt you at home and they hit you at school.
tor - tured and scared you for twen - ty odd years,
room at the top, they are tell - ing you still;

G

by giv - ing you no time in - stead of it all,
They hate you if you're clev - er and they de - spise a fool,
then they ex - pect you to pick a ca - reer,
but first you must learn how to smile as you kill

Am

till the pain is so big you feel
till you're so fuck - ing cra - zy you can
when you real - ly can't func - tion, you're
if you want to be like the

G ... Am

noth - ing at all.____
fol - low their rules.
so full of fear.
folks on the hill.____

A work - ing class

he - ro is some - thing to be.___

A

1 - 3

work - ing class he - ro is some - thing to be. ___

4, 5

2. They work - ing class he - ro is some - thing to be.___
3. When they've
4. Keep you

To Coda ⊕   D.S. 𝄋 (no repeats) al Coda ⊕   CODA ⊕

5. There's

If you want to be a he - ro, well, just fol - low me. ___

1

2

If you

57

DEAR YOKO
WORDS & MUSIC BY JOHN LENNON

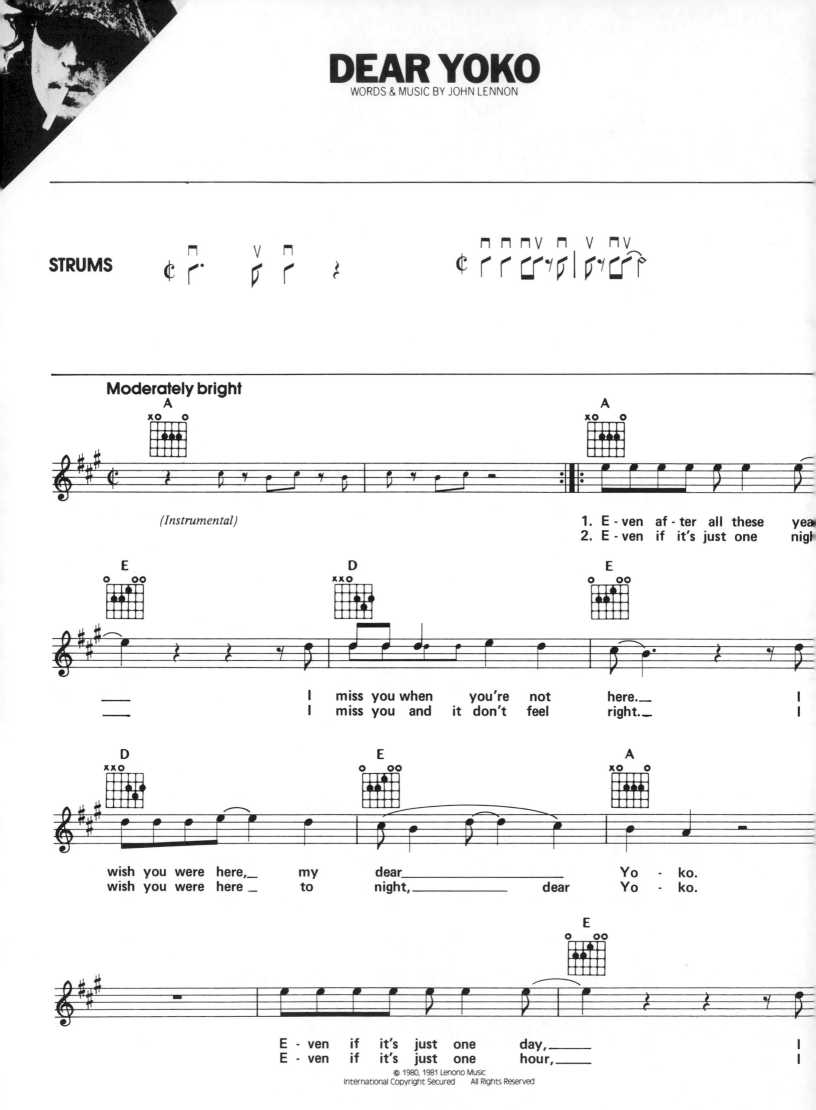

STRUMS

Moderately bright

(Instrumental)

1. E - ven af - ter all these yea
2. E - ven if it's just one nigh

I miss you when you're not here.__
I miss you and it don't feel right.__

wish you were here,__ my dear_____ Yo - ko.
wish you were here _ to night,_____ dear Yo - ko.

E - ven if it's just one day,_____
E - ven if it's just one hour,_____

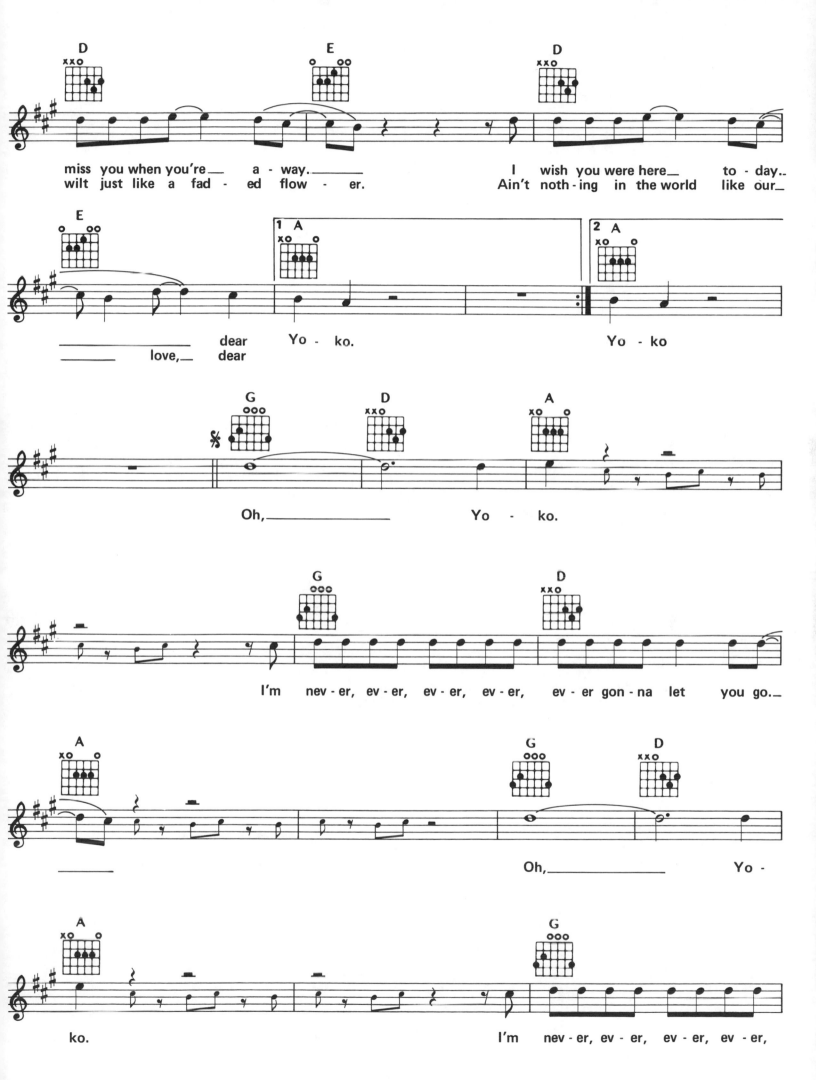

ev - er gon - na let you go.

3. E - ven when I'm miles at sea and
4. E - ven af - ter all this time, I

no - where is the place to be, your
miss you like the sun don't shine. With -

spir - it's watch - ing o - ver me, dear
out you I'm a one - track mind, dear

Yo - ko. E - ven when I watch T

V, there's a hole where you're sup - posed to be.

60

(JUST LIKE) STARTING OVER

WORDS & MUSIC BY JOHN LENNON

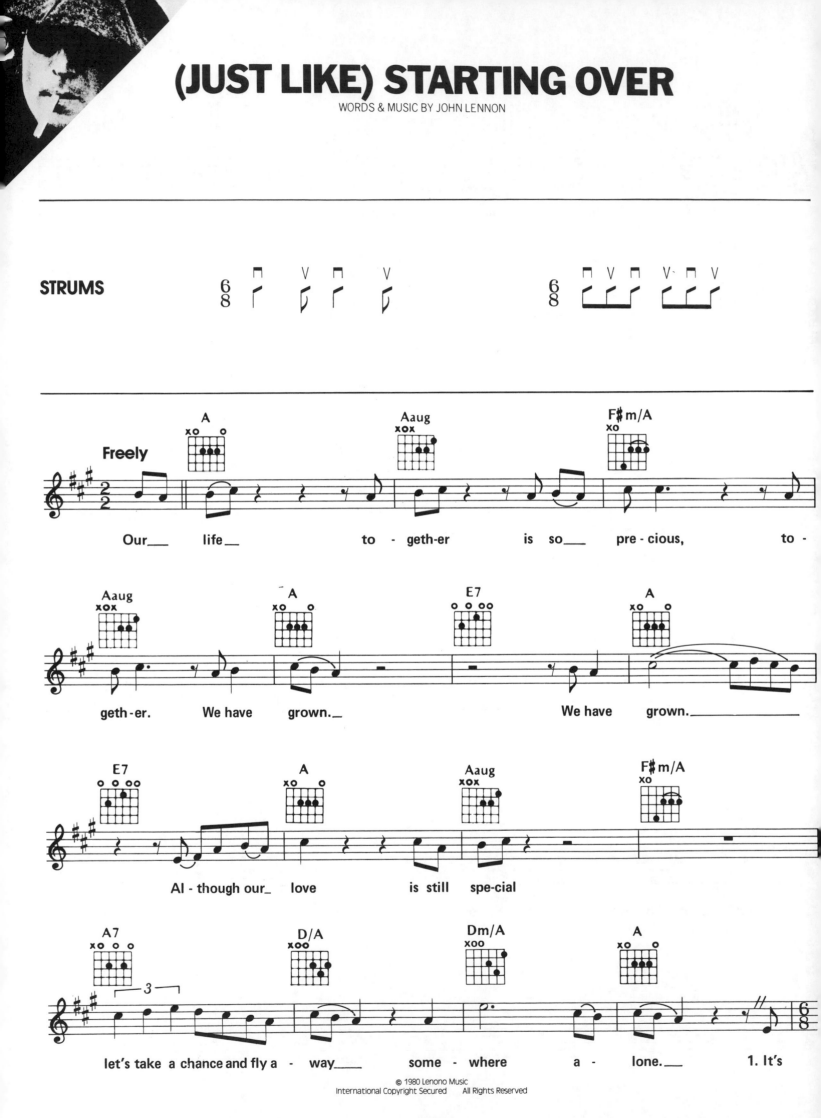

Moderately, with a strong beat

been too long since we took the time.___ No one's to blame. I
day we used to make it, love.___ Why can't we be

know time flies___ so quick - ly!
mak - in' love nice and eas - y?

But when I see you, dar - lin', it's
It's time to spread our wings and fly. Don't

like we both are fall - ing in love___ a - gain. It - 'll
let an - oth - er day go by,___ my love. It - 'll

be just like start - ing o - ver,
be just like start - ing o - ver,

start-ing o - ver.___
start-ing o - ver.___

2. Ev - 'ry

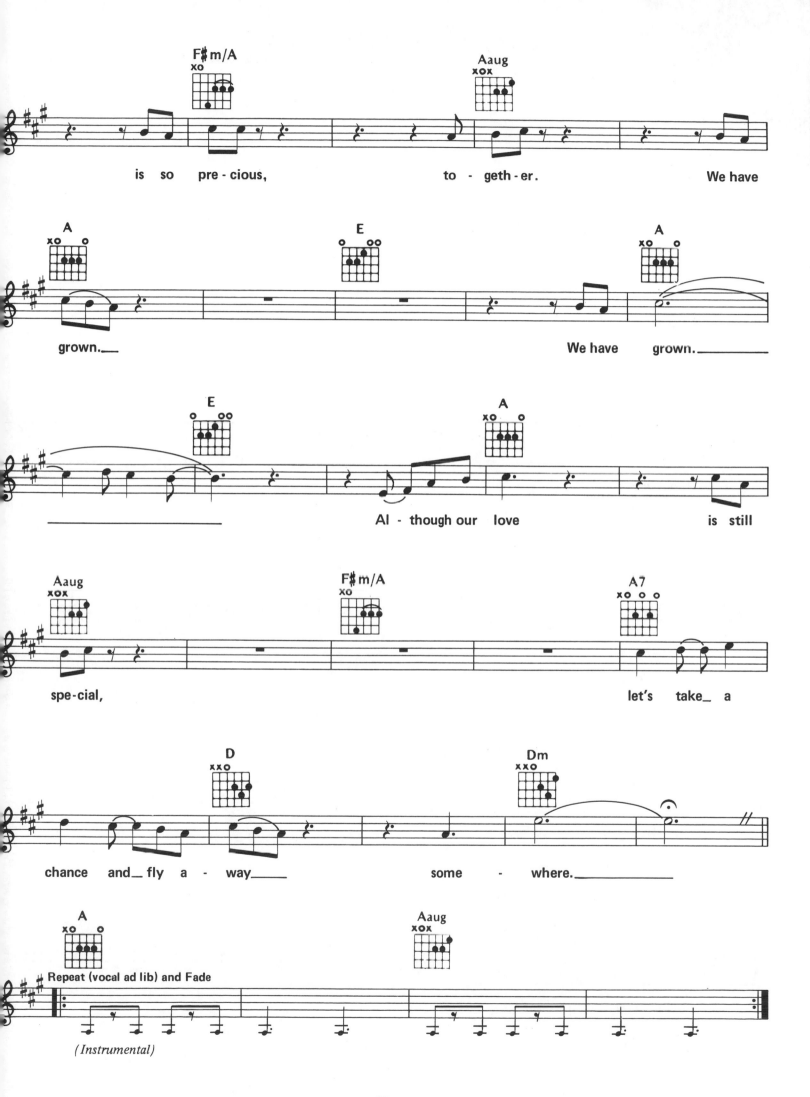

WELL, WELL, WELL

WORDS & MUSIC BY JOHN LENNON

STRUMS

Steady,
in 2

(Instrumental)

Well, well, well, oh,___ well.___

*Bass note only, in this rhythm:

Well, well, well,   oh,_____   well._____

1. I took my loved__ one out to
2.,4. I took my loved__ one to a
3. We sat and talked__ of rev - o -

din - ner   so we could get a bite to
big field   so we could watch the Eng - lish
lu - tion,   just like two li - b'rals in the

eat._____   And though we both__ had been much
sky._____   We both were ner - vous, feel - ing
sun._____   We talked of Wom - en's Lib - er -

thin - ner,   she looked so beau - ti - ful I could
guilt - y,   and neith - er one of us knew just
a - tion   and how the hell we could get things

eat her.   Well, well,   Well, well, well,
why.   Well, well,
done.

67

oh,_____ well._____ Well, well, well,

oh,_____ well._____ Well, well, well._____

Repeat ad lib (about 30 times)

_____ Oh,___ well.___ Well, well, well.___

F#*

___ *Bass only*

Guitar solo

BEAUTIFUL BOY (DARLING BOY)

WORDS & MUSIC BY JOHN LENNON

(Instrumental)

Close your eyes,— have no fear.— Th
go to sleep, say a lit-tle prayer.

mon- ster's gone.— He's on the run,— and your dad-dy's here.—
Ev- 'ry day,— in ev -'ry way,— it's get-ting bet-ter and bet-ter.

Beau- ti -ful, beau- ti -ful, beau- ti -ful, beau- ti -ful boy.___

CRIPPLED INSIDE

WORDS & MUSIC BY JOHN LENNON

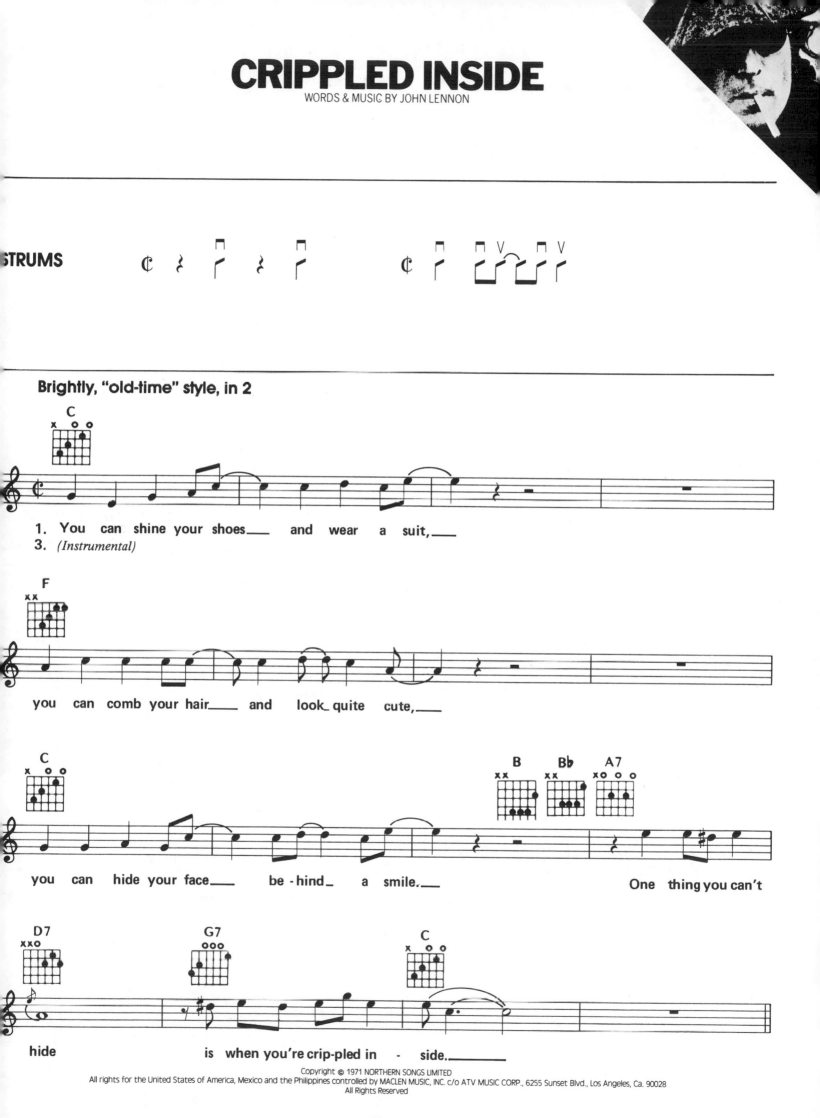

STRUMS

Brightly, "old-time" style, in 2

C

1. You can shine your shoes___ and wear a suit,___
3. *(Instrumental)*

F

you can comb your hair___ and look_ quite cute,___

C   B   Bb   A7

you can hide your face___ be-hind_ a smile.___   One thing you can't

D7   G7   C

hide   is when you're crip-pled in - side.___

2. You can wear a mask____ and paint your face,____
4. 5. You can go to church____ and sing a hymn,____

you can call your-self____ the hu - man race,____
you can judge me by____ the col - or of my skin,____

____ you can wear a col - lar and a tie..
____ you can live a lie____ un - til you die.

One thing you can't hide

To Coda ⊕

is when you're crip-pled in - side.____ Well now, you know that your ca

____ has nine lives, babe,____ nine lives

* Bass notes only

to it - self._____

G7   C

You on - ly got one____

Am7   C

____ and a dog's____ life ain't fun._____ Ma - ma, take a look__

G7   C

1   **2**   D.S. ℁ al Coda ⊕

out - side._____

CODA   C   B   Bb   A7   D7

side.__   One   thing you can't   hide

Slowly, in 4 (♩♩ = ♪³♪)

G7   C   B   Bb   A7   D7

is when you're crip-pled in - side.__   One__ thing you can't   hide

G   C   C7   F   Ab7   G7   Eb9   C9

is when you're crip-pled in - side.__

(Bass run, octave higher)

75

OH MY LOVE

WORDS & MUSIC BY JOHN LENNON AND YOKO ONO

FINGER PICKS

Gently

1. Oh, my____ love,____ for the first____ time in my life____
2. Oh, my____ love,____ for the first____ time in my life____

my_____ eyes____ are wide op - pen.
my_____ mind____ is wide op - pen.

Oh, my____ lov - er, for the first____ time in my life____
Oh, my____ lov - er, for the first____ time in my life____

my____ eyes can____ see.
my____ mind can____ feel.

I   see the wind,___ oh,___ I   see the trees;____
I   feel____ sor-row, oh,___ I   feel____ dreams;__

ev - 'ry - thing is clear___ in my heart.
ev - 'ry - thing is clear___ in my heart.

I   see the clouds,__ oh,___ I   see the sky;_____
I   feel____ life,___ oh,___ I   feel____ love;____

ev - 'ry - thing is clear___ in our world.
ev - 'ry - thing is clear___ in our world.

(Instrumental)

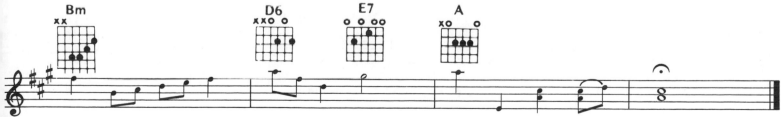

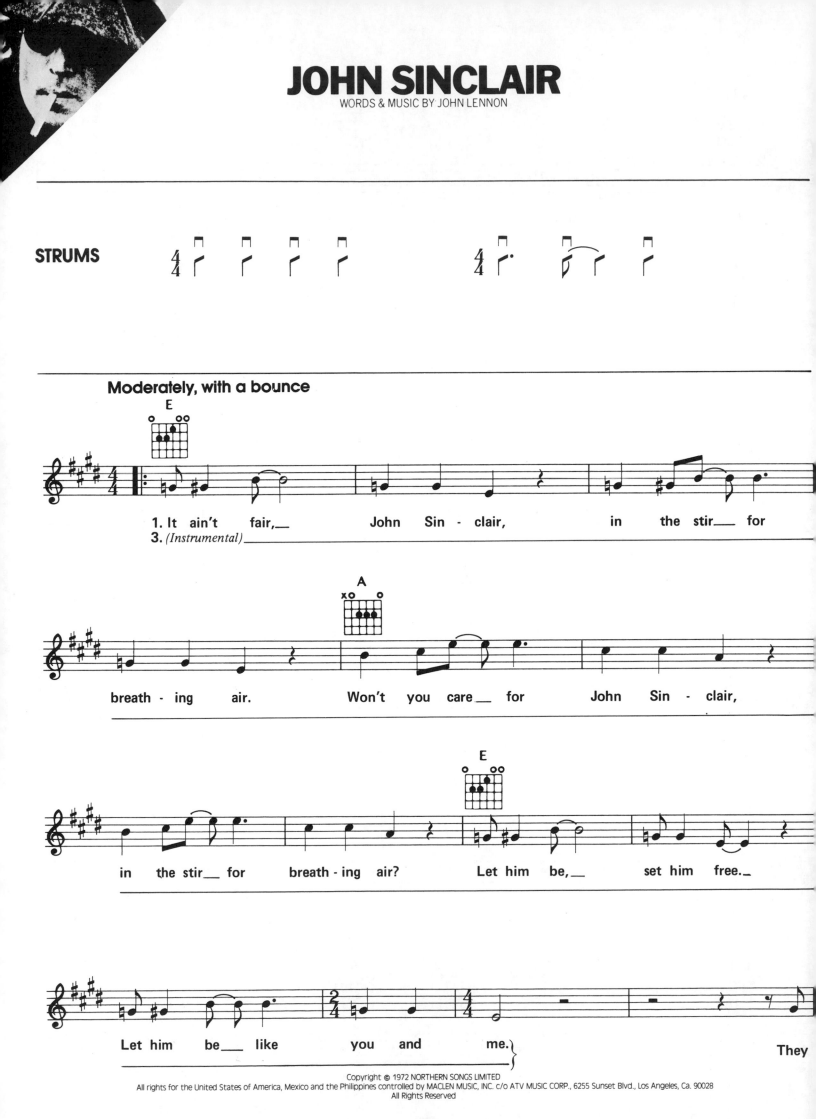

JOHN SINCLAIR
WORDS & MUSIC BY JOHN LENNON

STRUMS

Moderately, with a bounce

1. It ain't fair,__ John Sin - clair, in the stir__ for
3. (Instrumental)__

breath - ing air. Won't you care__ for John Sin - clair,

in the stir__ for breath - ing air? Let him be,__ set him free.__

Let him be__ like you and me.

They

mak - ing hay, he'd be free,___ they'd let him be,
of the man. Let him be,___ lift the lid,

breath - ing air___ like you and me. Right on.___ } They
bring him to___ his wife and kids.

gave him ten___ for two;___ { what else can___ the judg-es do?___ } We
{ what else can___ the bas-tards do?___ }

got - ta, got - ta, got - ta, got - ta, got - ta, got - ta, got - ta, got - ta,

got - ta, got - ta, got - ta, got - ta, got - ta, got - ta, got - ta, set___ him

Repeat and Fade

free.   (Instrumental)

BEAUTIFUL BOYS

WORDS & MUSIC BY YOKO ONO

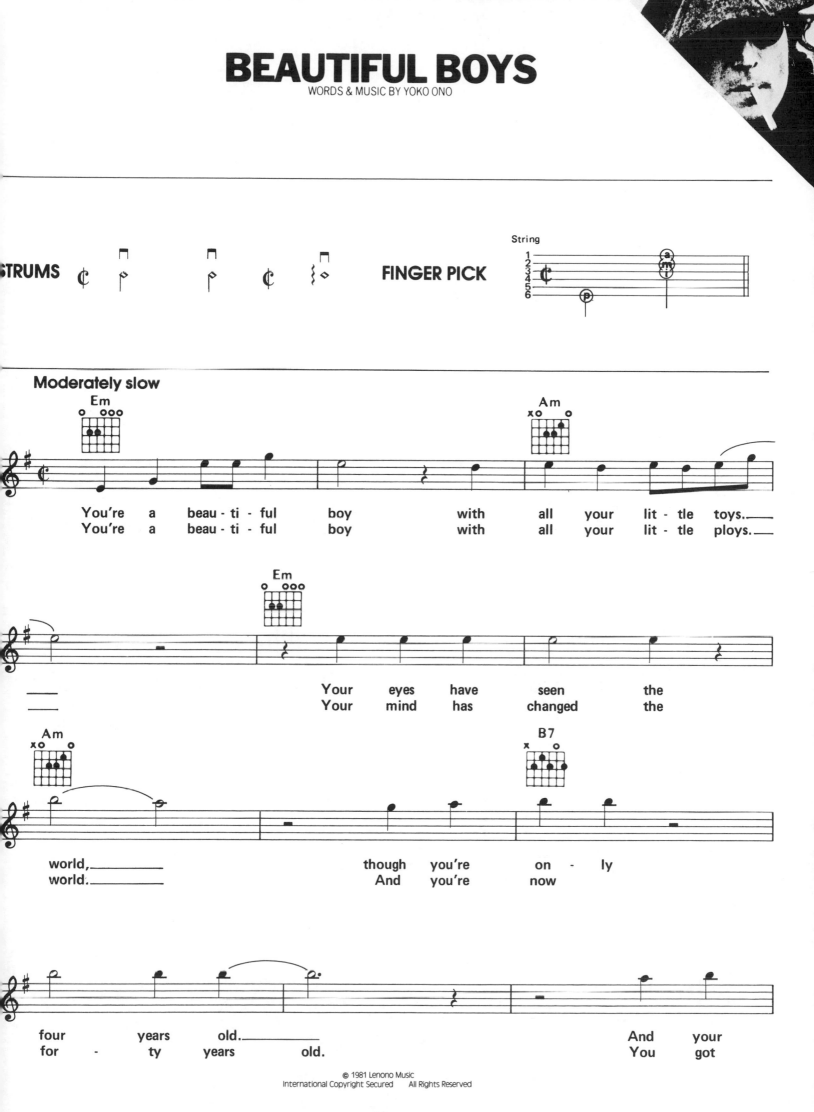

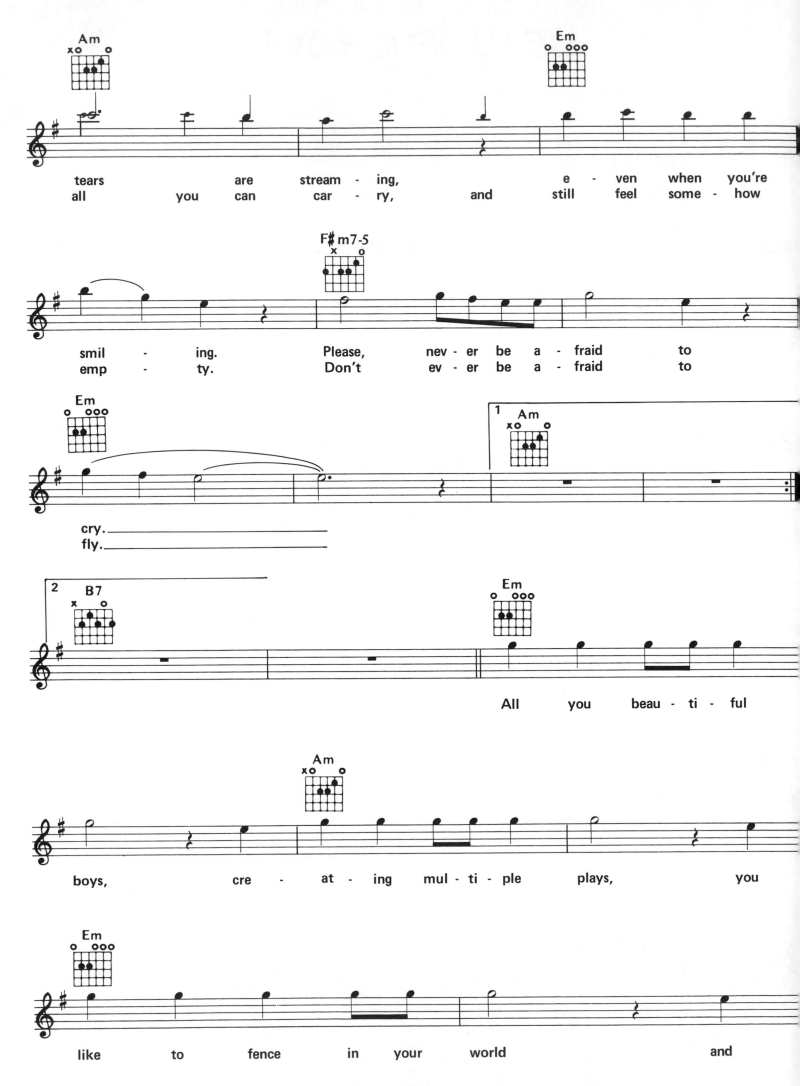

set - tle down when you're old. You can run from

pole to pole and nev - er scratch your soul.

Don't be a - fraid to go to hell and back.____

Don't be a - fraid to be____ a -

fraid.____ *(Instrumental)*

I FOUND OUT

WORDS & MUSIC BY JOHN LENNON

Moderately

No Chords (Bass play melody two octaves lower)

I told you be - fore,— stay a - way from my door.— Don't give me that

broth - er, broth - er, broth - er, broth - er. The freaks on the phone,

___ won't leave me a - lone,_____ so don't give me that broth-er, broth-er,broth-er,broth

No!___ I, I found out.___ I, I found out.___

1. Now that I showed_ you what I been through,_ don't take no-bod-y's word_

* Single Bass notes only throughout.

Additional Lyrics

2. Some of you sitting there with your cock in your hand;
Don't get you nowhere, don't make you a man.
I heard something 'bout my ma and my pa;
They didn't want me so they made me a star.
(REFRAIN)

3. Old Hare Krishna got nothing on you,
Just keep you crazy with nothing to do.
Keep you occupied with pie in the sky;
There ain't no guru who can see through your eyes.
(REFRAIN)

4. I seen through junkies, I been through it all;
I seen religion from Jesus to Paul.
Don't let them fool you with dope and cocaine;
No one can harm you, feel your own pain.
(REFRAIN)

HAPPY XMAS (WAR IS OVER)

WORDS & MUSIC BY JOHN LENNON AND YOKO ONO

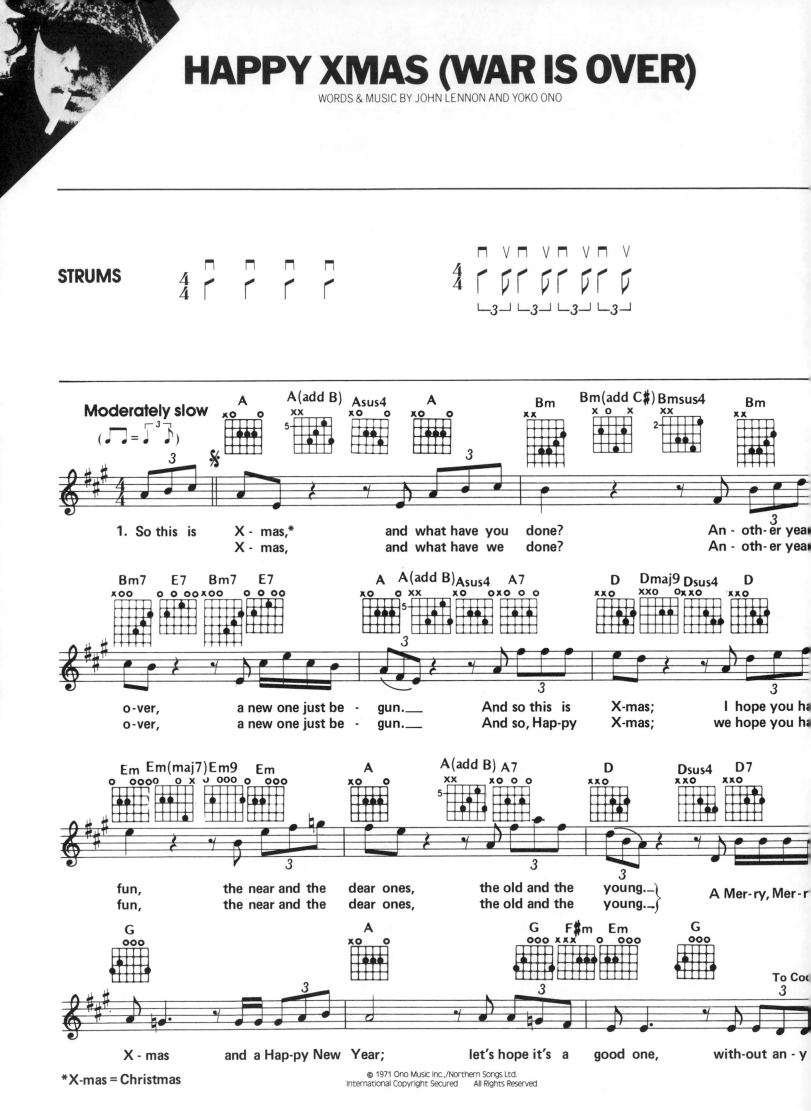

*X-mas = Christmas

JEALOUS GUY
WORDS & MUSIC BY JOHN LENNON

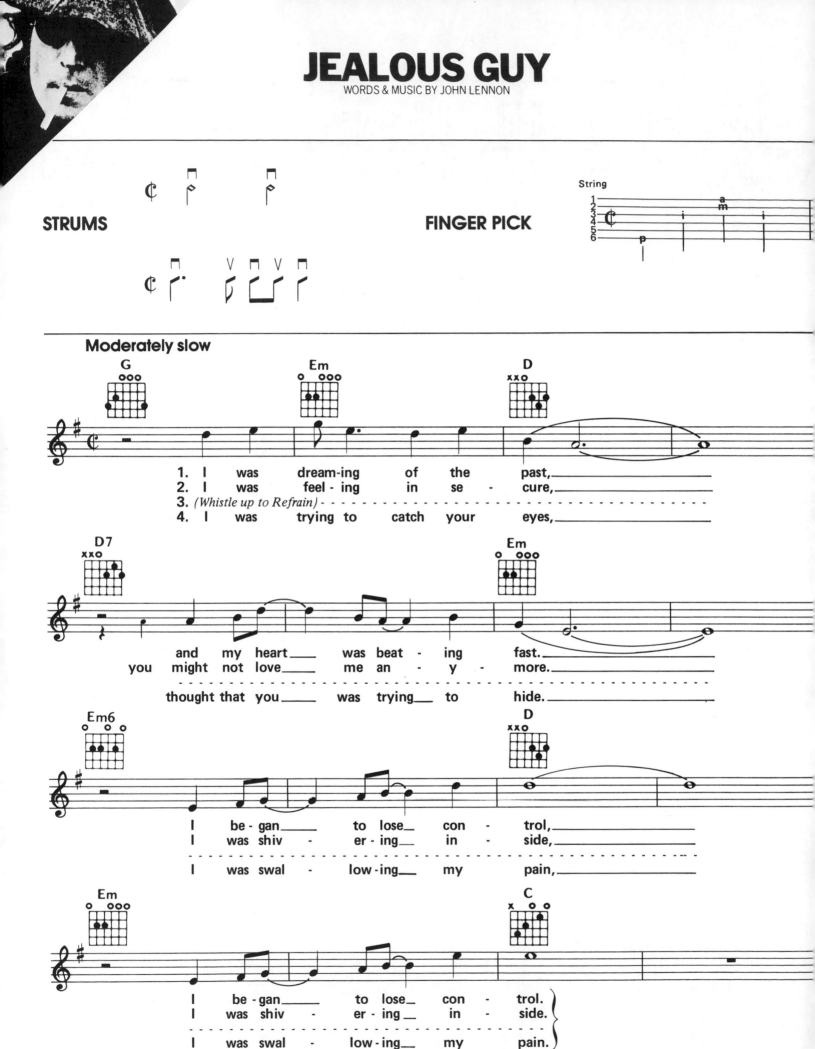

STRUMS

FINGER PICK

Moderately slow

G   Em   D

1. I was dream-ing of the past,_____
2. I was feel-ing in se - cure,_____
3. *(Whistle up to Refrain)* - - - - - - - -
4. I was trying to catch your eyes,_____

D7   Em

and my heart____ was beat - ing fast._____
you might not love____ me an - y - more._____
- -
thought that you____ was trying____ to hide._____

Em6   D

I be - gan____ to lose____ con - trol,_____
I was shiv - er - ing____ in - side,_____
I was swal - low-ing____ my pain,_____

Em   C

I be - gan____ to lose____ con - trol.
I was shiv - er - ing____ in - side.
I was swal - low-ing____ my pain.

I did-n't mean to hurt_____ you._____

I'm sor-ry that_____ I made you cry,_____ oh no.

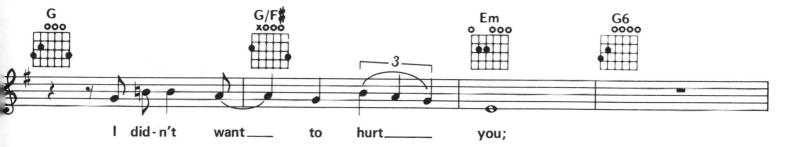

I did-n't want_____ to hurt_____ you;

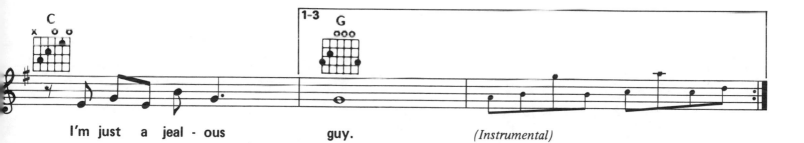

I'm just a jeal-ous guy. *(Instrumental)*

guy._____ Watch out, I'm just a jeal-ous guy._____ Look out,_____ babe._____

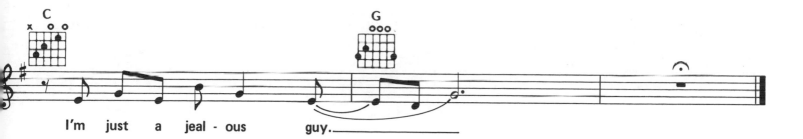

I'm just a jeal-ous guy._____

89

LOOK AT ME
WORDS & MUSIC BY JOHN LENNON

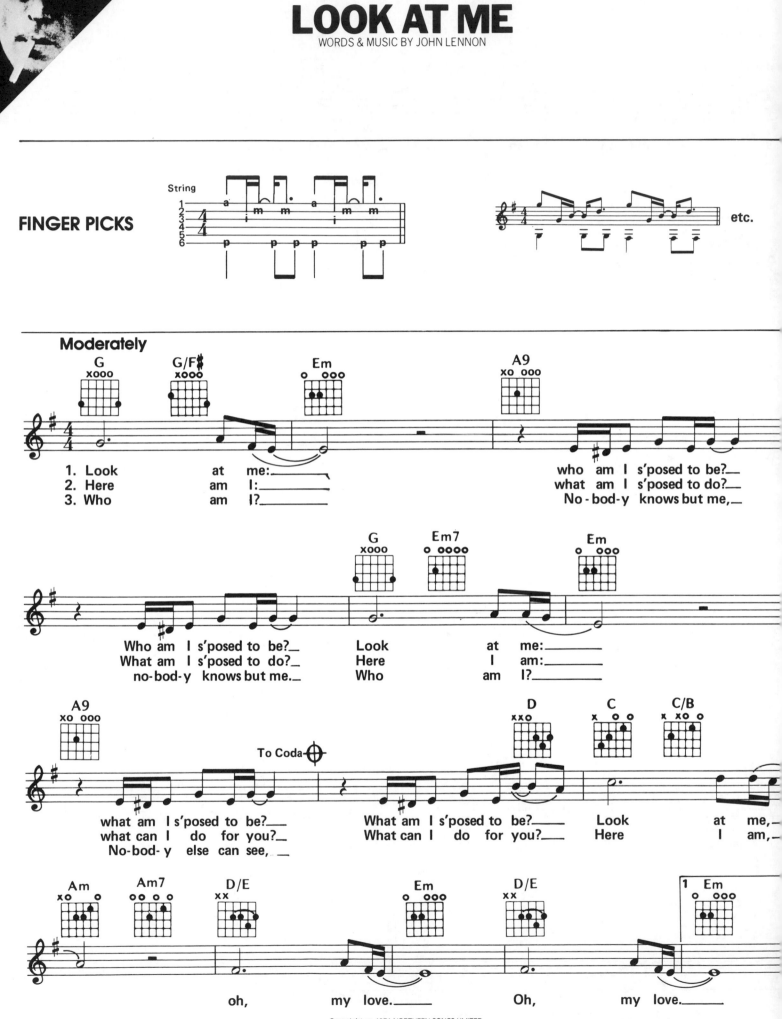

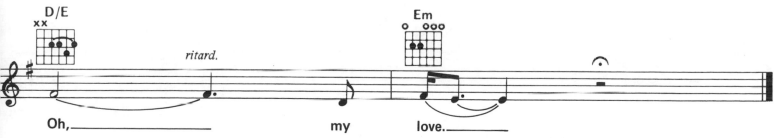

IT'S SO HARD

WORDS & MUSIC BY JOHN LENNON

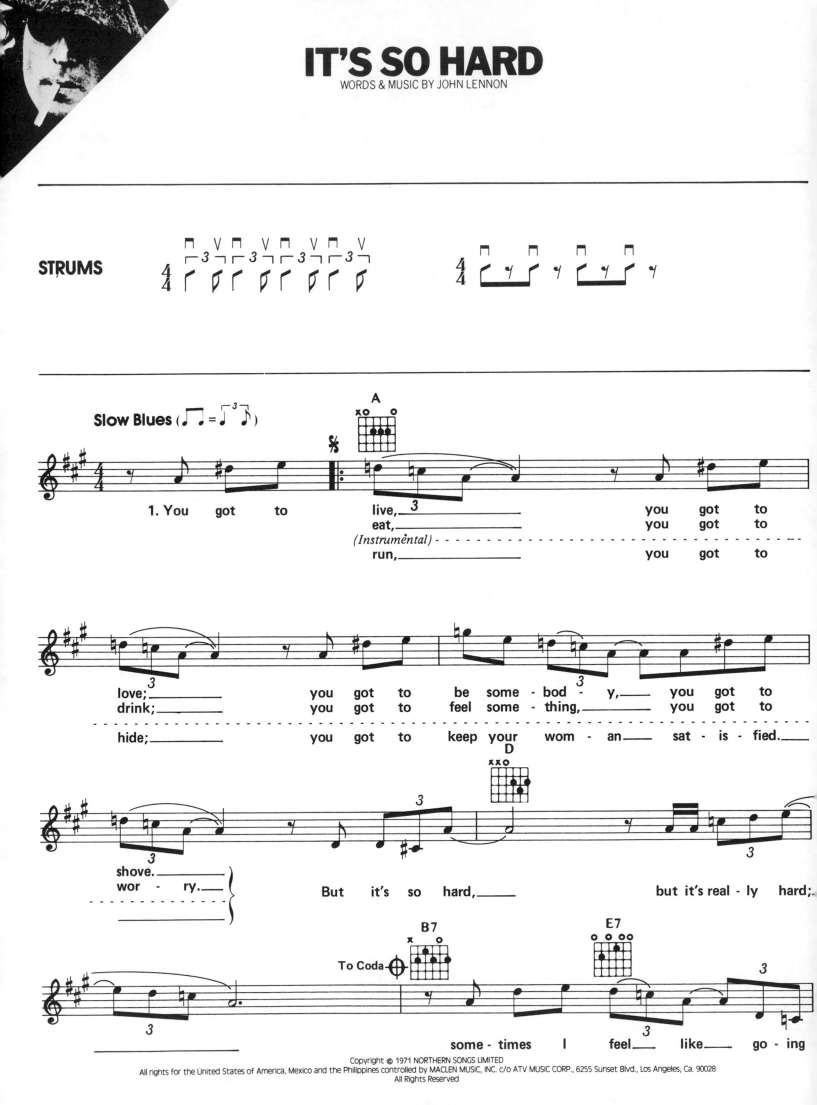

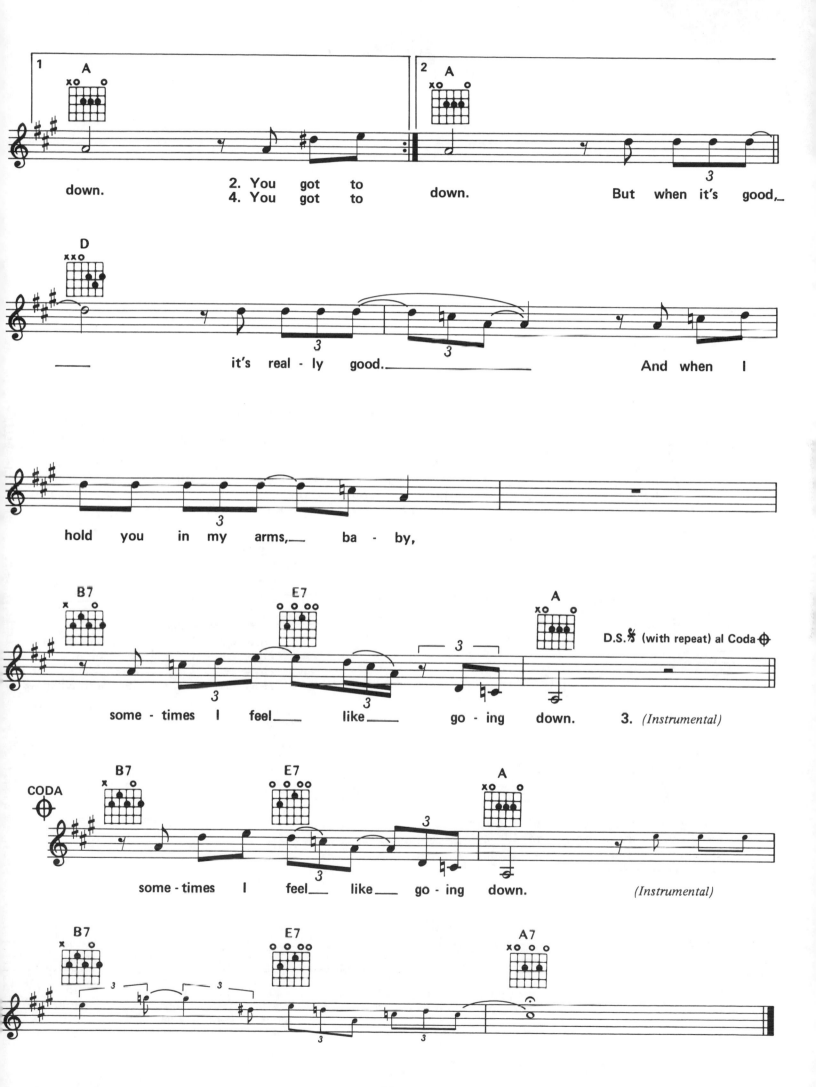

HOW

WORDS & MUSIC BY JOHN LENNON

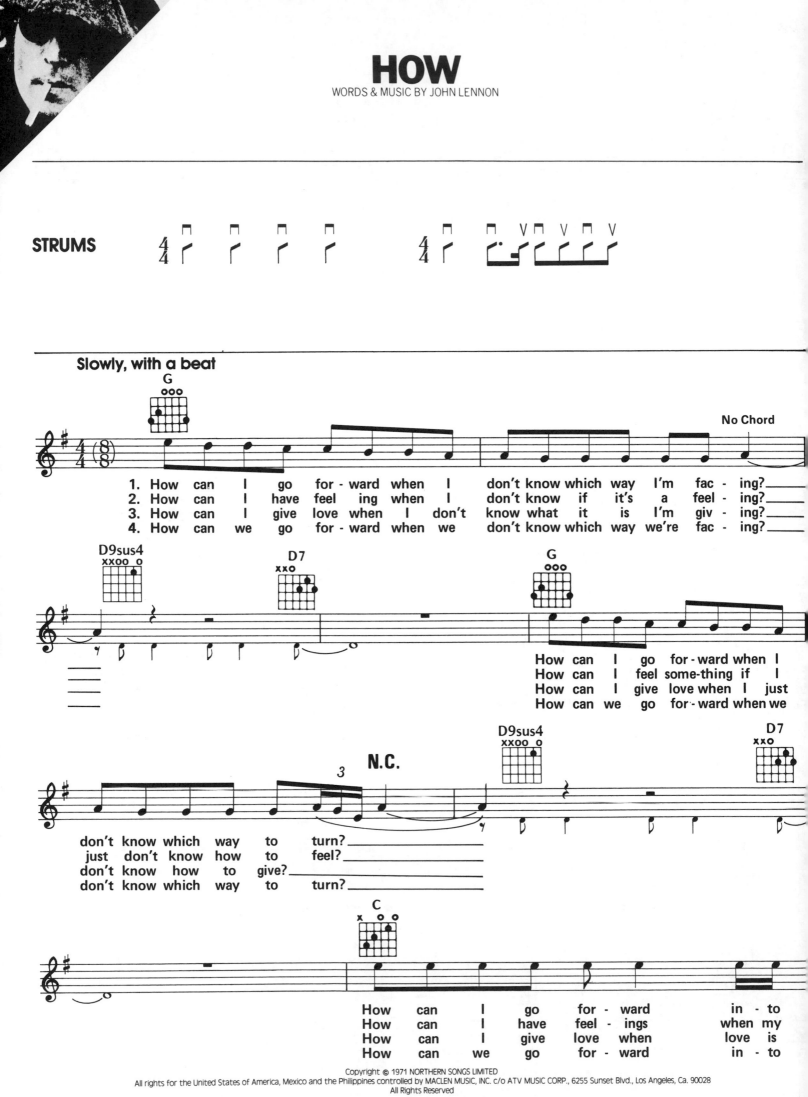

some-thing I'm not sure of? _____
feel-ings have al-ways been de-nied? _____
some-thing I ain't nev-er had? _____
some-thing we're not sure of? _____

Oh, no.   Oh,

no.   You know;

life can be long and you got to be so strong, and the

world { is so } { she is } tough;   some-times I feel I've had e-nough.

95

GIMME SOME TRUTH

WORDS & MUSIC BY JOHN LENNON

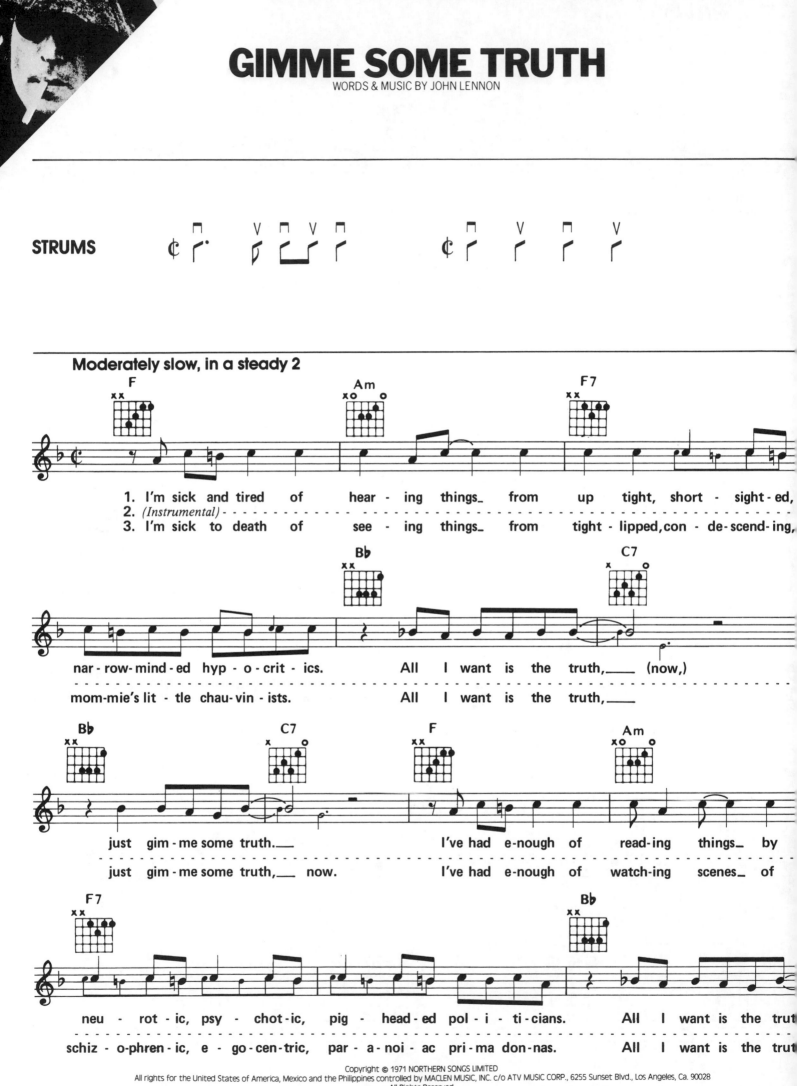

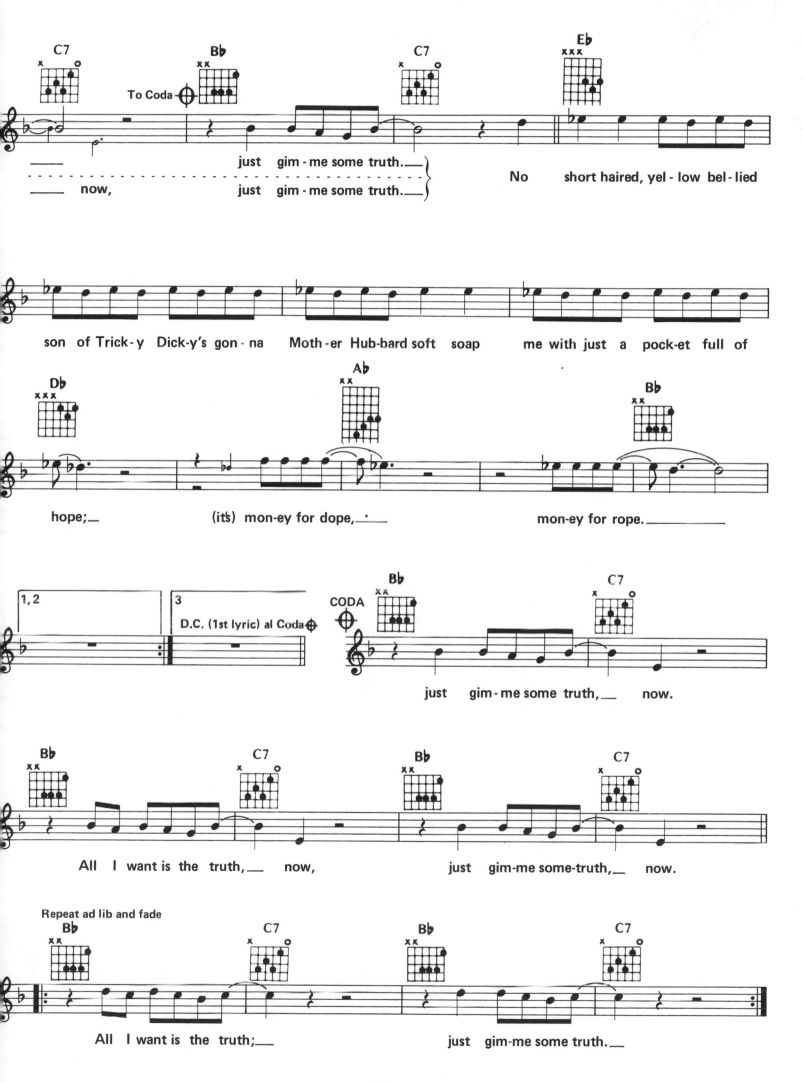

OH YOKO
WORDS & MUSIC BY JOHN LENNON

STRUMS

FINGER PICK

Brightly, in 2

1. In the mid - dle of the night,
2. In the mid - dle of a bath,
3. In the mid - dle of a shave,
4. In the mid - dle of a dream,
5. In the mid - dle of a cloud,

in the mid-dle of the night I call___ your name.___
in the mid-dle of a bath I call___ your name.___
in the mid-dle of a shave I call___ your name.___
in the mid-dle of a dream I call___ your name.___
in the mid-dle of a cloud I call___ your name.___

Oh, Yo - ko.___

Oh, Yo - ko.___ My

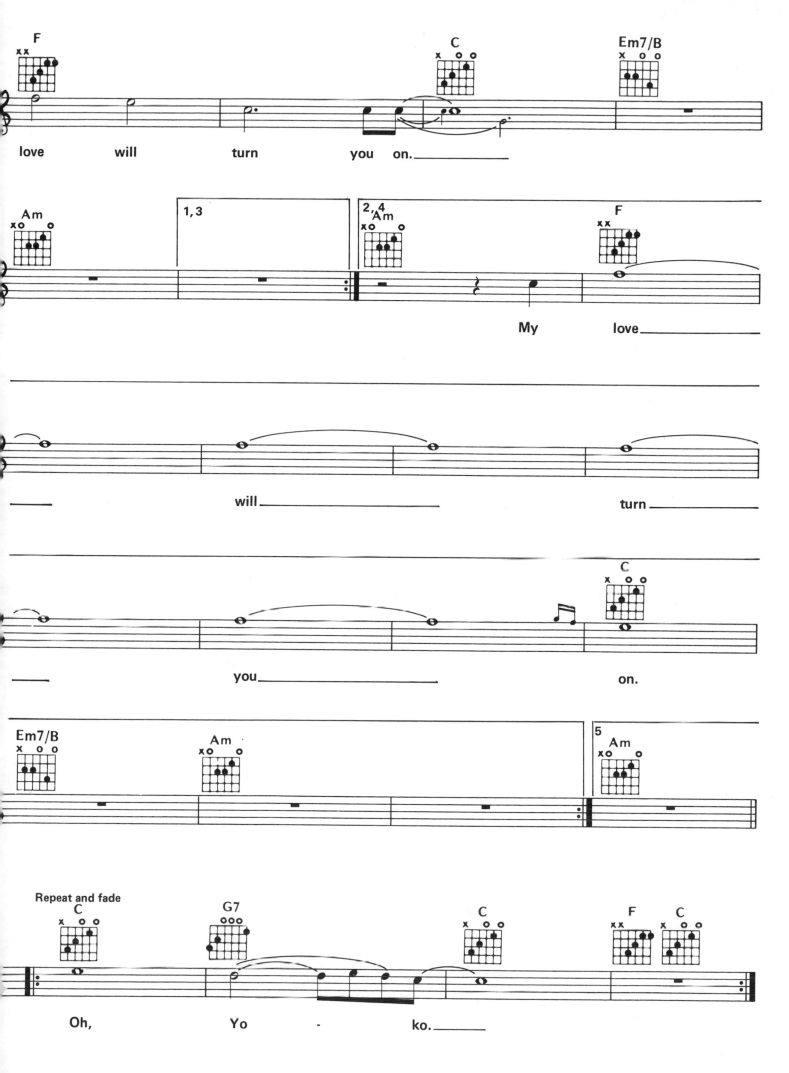

love   will   turn   you   on._____

1, 3

2, 4

My   love_____

will_____   turn_____

you_____   on.

Repeat and fade

Oh,   Yo - ko._____

CLEAN UP TIME
WORDS & MUSIC BY JOHN LENNON

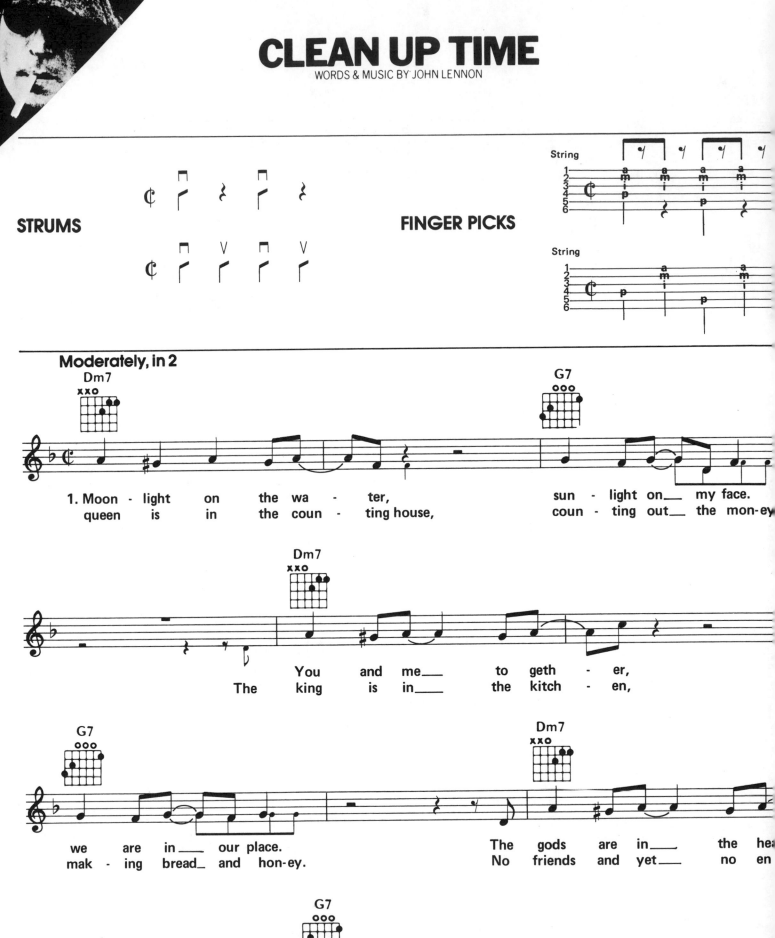

STRUMS

FINGER PICKS

Moderately, in 2

Dm7

G7

1. Moon - light on the wa - ter, sun - light on__ my face.
queen is in the coun - ting house, coun - ting out__ the mon-ey

Dm7

The You and me__ to geth - er,
The king is in__ the kitch - en,

G7

Dm7

we are in __ our place.
mak - ing bread_ and hon-ey.

The gods are in __ the hea
No friends and yet__ no en

G7

ens, the an - gels treat__ us well.__ Th
e - mies, ab - so - lute - ly free.__ No

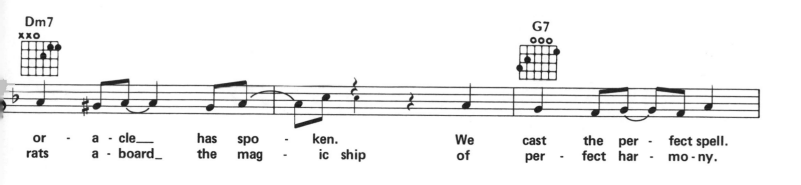

or - a - cle___ has spo - ken.   We   cast   the per - fect spell.
rats   a - board_   the mag -   ic ship   of   per - fect har - mo - ny.

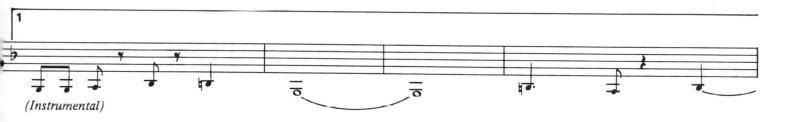

(Instrumental)

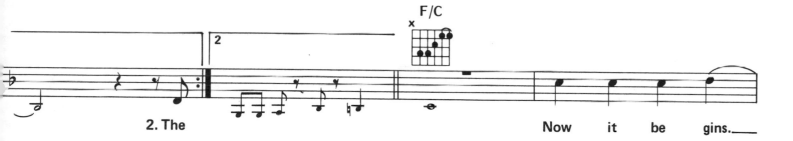

2. The   Now   it   be   gins.___

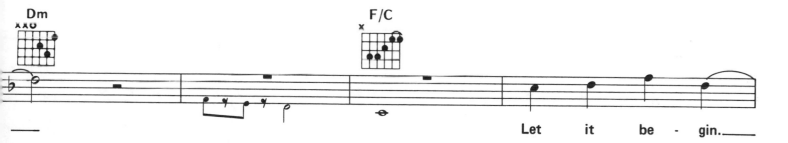

Let   it   be - gin.___

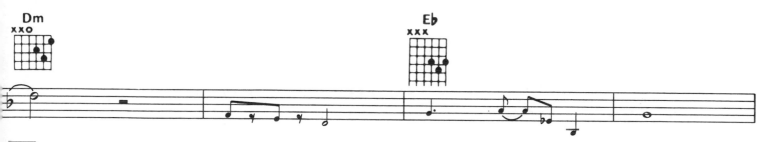

Clean - up   time.___

Well,

well,

well._____

3. How - ev - er far____ we trav - el, wher

ev - er we___ may roam, the cen - ter of___ the cir

- cle will al - ways be___ our home.___

Repeat and Fade

Clean - up time._____

SUNDAY, BLOODY SUNDAY

WORDS & MUSIC BY JOHN LENNON AND YOKO ONO

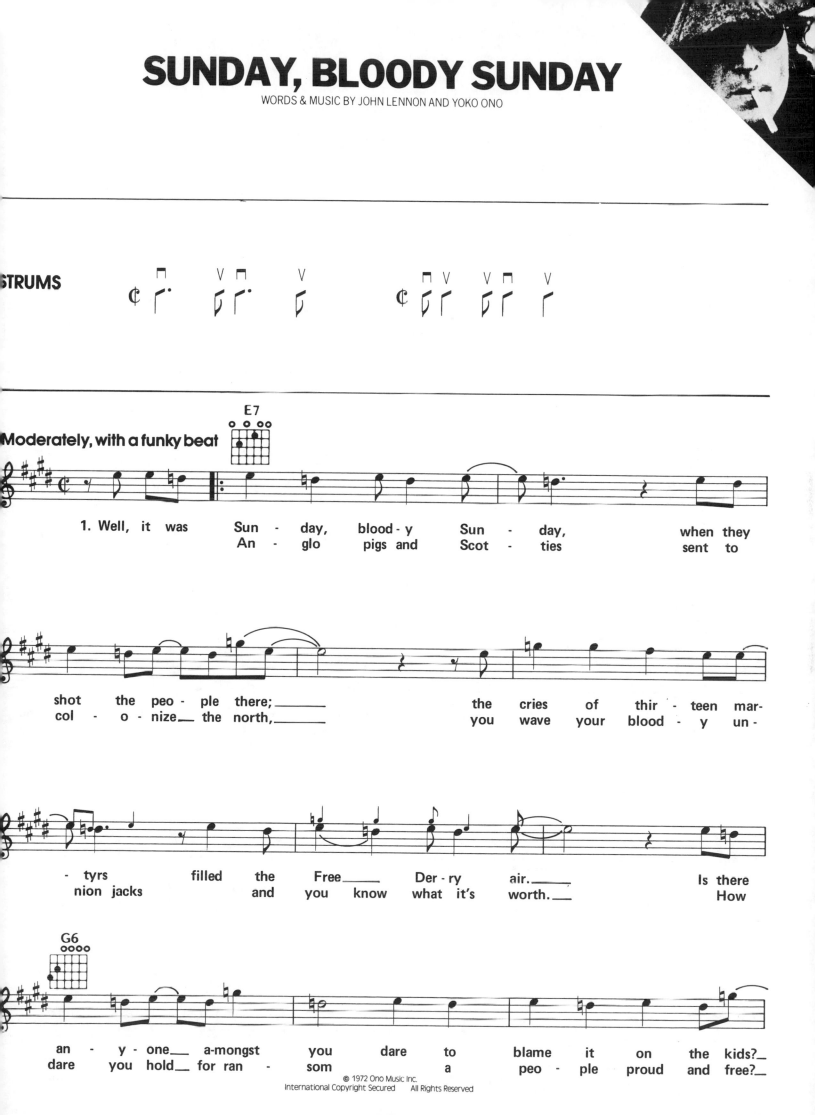

1. Well, it was Sun - day, blood - y Sun - day, when they
An - glo pigs and Scot - ties sent to

shot the peo - ple there; the cries of thir - teen mar -
col - o - nize the north, you wave your blood - y un -

- tyrs filled the Free Der - ry air. Is there
nion jacks and you know what it's worth. How

an - y - one a-mongst you dare to blame it on the kids?
dare you hold for ran - som a peo - ple proud and free?

Not a sol - dier boy was bleed - ing when they
Keep Ire - land for the I - rish, put the

nailed the cof - fin lids!_____ Sun - day, blood-y Sun-
Eng - lish back to sea!_____

day, blood - y Sun - day's the

day._____ 2. You claim to be___ ma - jor - i - ty; well, you
4. It's al - ways blood - y Sun - day in the

know that it's___ a lie._____ You're real - ly a mi - nor -
con - cen - tra - tion camps._____ Keep Falls Road free for - ev -

- i - ty on this sweet em - 'rald isle.___ When
- er from the blood - y Eng - lish hands.___ Re -

104

Stor - mont bans our march - es, they've got a lot ___ to learn; ___
pa - tri - ate to Brit - ain, all of you who call it home. ___

___ in - tern - ment is no an - swer, it's those
___ Leave Ire - land to the I - rish, not for

moth-er's turn to burn! ___ Sun - day, blood-y Sun-
Lon - don or for Rome!

day, blood-y Sun - day's the day!

Repeat and Fade

1.
2.

3. You Sun - day, blood-y Sun -

day, blood-y Sun - day's the day!

I DON'T WANNA BE A SOLDIER

WORDS & MUSIC BY JOHN LENNON

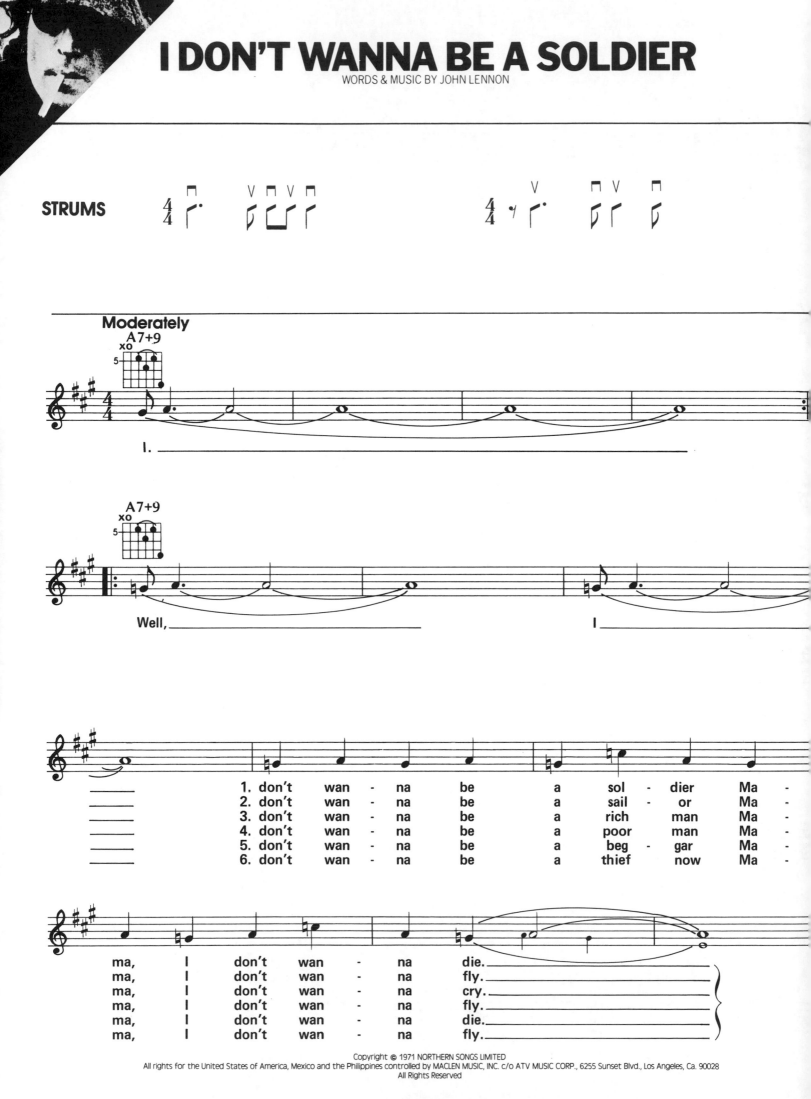

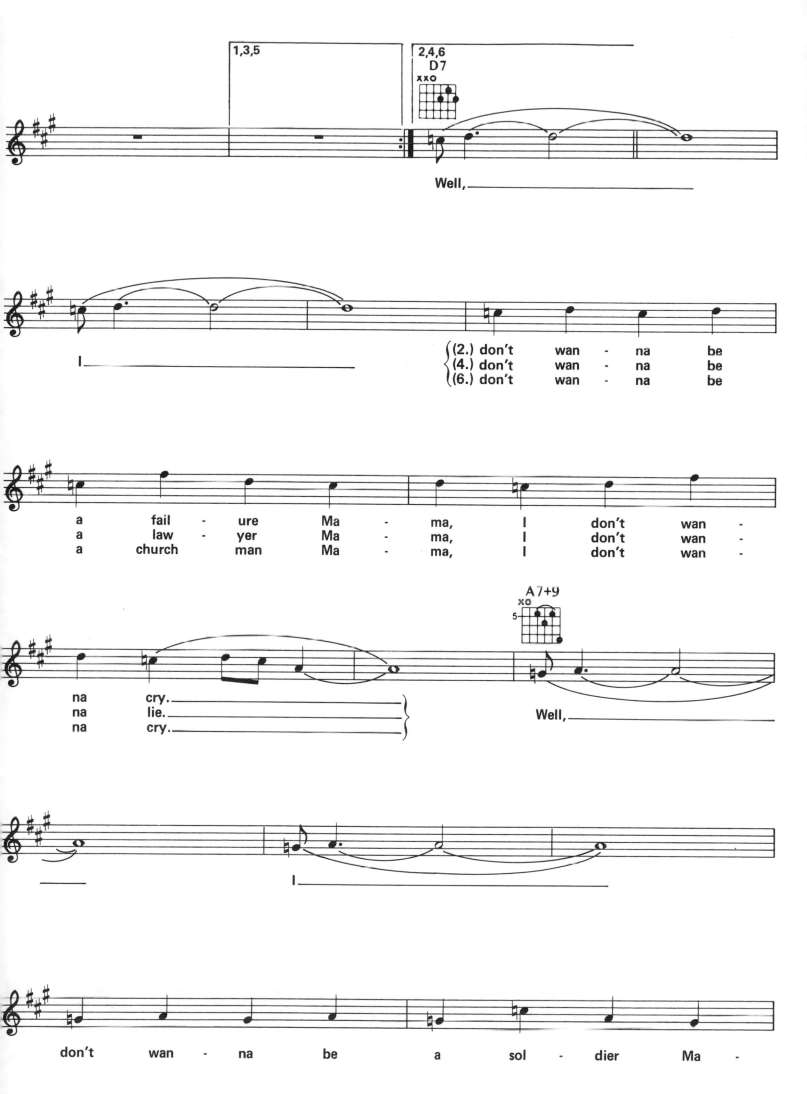

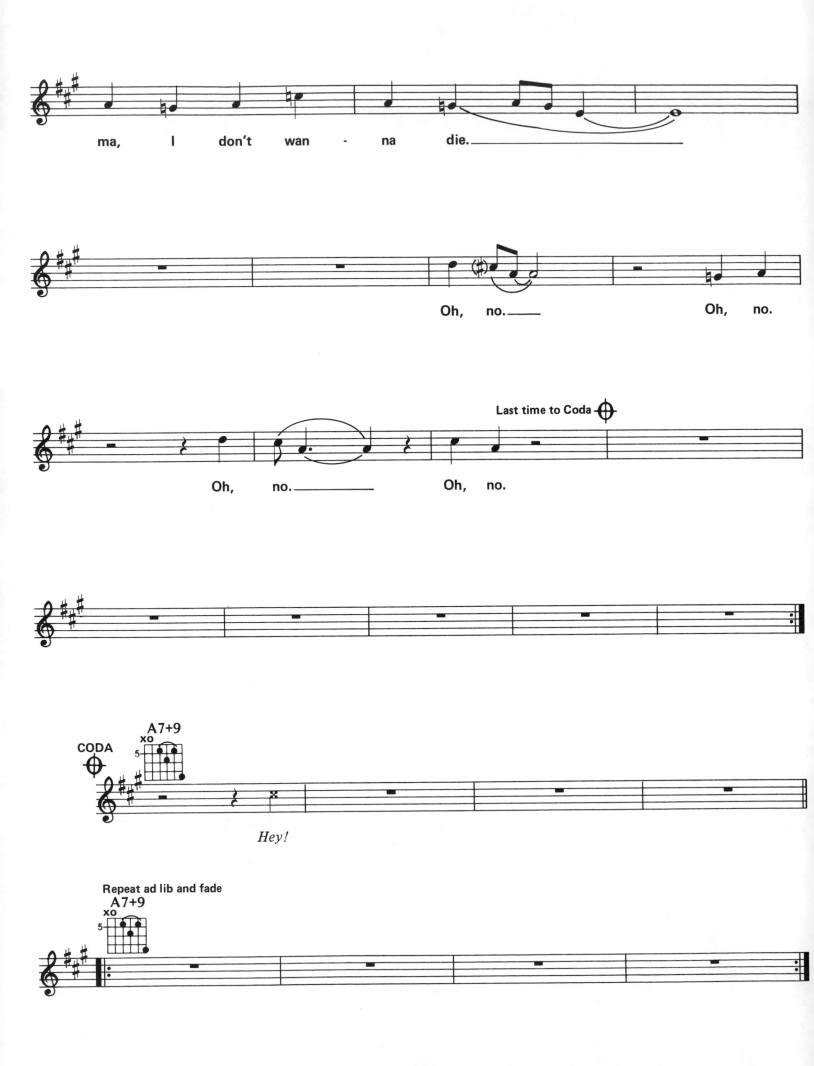

ma, I don't wan - na die._____

Oh, no.___   Oh, no.

Oh, no.___   Oh, no.

Last time to Coda ⊕

CODA ⊕

A7+9

Hey!

Repeat ad lib and fade

A7+9

I'M MOVING ON

WORDS & MUSIC BY YOKO ONO

Save your sweet talk   for   when you score,

keep your Mon-day kiss - es   for your glass la - dy.

I want the truth___ and noth-ing more.___

I'm mov-ing on,___ mov-ing on.___ you're get-ting pho - ny.___

(Instrumental) You did-n't have to tell a white

lie. You know you scored me for life.___

Don't stick your fin-ger in my pie. You know I see through your

jive.___ I want the truth and noth-ing more.__

I'm mov-ing on,___ mov-ing on.___ We're get-ting

pho-ny.___ *(Instrumental)*

When you were an-gry you had love in your eyes.

When you were sad,___ you had dream in your voice.

Now you're giv - ing me your win - dow___

smile.___ I'm mov - ing on,___ mov - ing on.___ It's get - ting

pho - ny.___ *(Instrumental)*

Repeat and fade

Your Favorite Music For Guitar
Made Easy

American Folksongs for Easy Guitar

Over 70 songs, including: All The Pretty Little Horses • Animal Fair • Aura Lee • Billy Boy • Buffalo Gals (Won't You Come Out Tonight) • Bury Me Not On The Lone Prairie • Camptown Races • (Oh, My Darling) Clementine • (I Wish I Was In) Dixie • The Drunken Sailor • Franky And Johnny • Home On The Range • Hush, Little Baby • I've Been Working On The Railroad • Jacob's Ladder • John Henry • My Old Kentucky Home • She'll Be Comin' Round The Mountain • Shenandoah • Simple Gifts • Swing Low, Sweet Chariot • The Wabash Cannon Ball • When Johnny Comes Marching Home • and more!
00702031 ....$9.95

The Big Christmas Collection

An outstanding collection of 100 Christmas tunes that even beginners can enjoy. Songs include: Away In A Manger • The Chipmunk Song • Deck The Hall • Feliz Navidad • Frosty The Snow Man • Fum, Fum, Fum • Grandma's Killer Fruitcake • Happy Holiday • It's Beginning To Look Like Christmas • Rudolph, The Red-Nosed Reindeer • Silent Night • Silver Bells • You're All I Want For Christmas • and more.
00698978 ....$14.95

The Broadway Book

Over 100 favorite show tunes including: All I Ask Of You • Beauty And The Beast • Cabaret • Edelweiss • I Whistle A Happy Tune • Memory • One • People • Sound Of Music • Tomorrow • With One Look • and more.
00702015 ...$14.95

The Big Book of Children's Songs

Over 60 songs, including: Are You Sleeping • The Bare Necessities • Beauty And The Beast • The Brady Bunch • The Candy Man • Casper The Friendly Ghost • Edelweiss • Feed The Birds • (Meet) The Flintstones • Happy Trails • Heigh Ho • I'm Popeye The Sailor Man • Jesus Loves Me • The Muffin Man • On Top Of Spaghetti • Puff The Magic Dragon • A Spoonful Of Sugar • Zip-A-Dee-Doo-Dah • and more.
00702027 ....$12.95

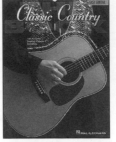

The Classic Country Book

Over 100 favorite country hits including: Another Somebody Done Somebody Wrong Song • Could I Have This Dance • Don't It Make My Brown Eyes Blue • Elvira • Folsom Prison Blues • The Gambler • Heartaches By The Number • I Fall To Pieces • Kiss An Angel Good Mornin' • Lucille • The Most Beautiful Girl In The World • Oh, Lonesome Me • Rocky Top • Sixteen Tons • Tumbling Tumbleweeds • Will The Circle Be Unbroken • You Needed Me • and more.
00702018 ....$19.95

The Classic Rock Book

89 monumental songs from the '60's, '70's and '80's, such as: American Woman • Born To Be Wild • Cocaine • Dust In The Wind • Fly Like An Eagle • Gimme Three Steps • I Can See For Miles • Layla • Magic Carpet Ride • Reelin' In The Years • Sweet Home Alabama • Tumbling Dice • Walk This Way • You Really Got Me • and more.
00698977 ....$19.95

National Anthems For Easy Guitar

50 official national anthems in their original language, complete with strum and pick patterns and chord frames. Countries represented include Australia, Brazil, Canada, Cuba, France, Germany, Great Britain, Haiti, Irish Republic, Mexico, Peru, Poland, Russia, Sweden, United States of America, and more.
00702025 ....$12.95

The New Country Hits Book

100 hot country hits including: Achy Breaky Heart • Ain't Going Down ('Til The Sun Comes Up) • Blame It On Your Heart • Boot Scootin' Boogie • Chattahoochee • Don't Rock The Jukebox • Friends In Low Places • Honky Tonk Attitude • I Feel Lucky • I Take My Chances • Little Less Talk And A Lot More Action • Mercury Blues • One More Last Chance • Somewhere In My Broken Heart • T-R-O-U-B-L-E • The Whiskey Ain't Workin' • and more.
00702017 ....$19.95

FOR MORE INFORMATION, SEE YOUR LOCAL MUSIC DEALER, OR WRITE TO:

HAL•LEONARD® CORPORATION

7777 W. BLUEMOUND RD. P.O. BOX 13819 MILWAUKEE, WI 53213

Contact Hal Leonard on the internet at http://www.halleonard.com

Prices, contents, and availability subject to change without notice. Some products may not be available outside the U.S.A.